Romeo and Juliet

ARDEN STUDENT SKILLS: LANGUAGE AND WRITING

Series Editor:

Dymphna Callaghan, Syracuse University

Published Titles

The Tempest, Brinda Charry
Macbeth, Emma Smith

Forthcoming Titles

Hamlet, Dympna Callaghan
Othello, Laurie Maguire
Twelfth Night, Frances E. Dolan
King Lear, Jean Howard
A Midsummer Night's Dream, Heidi Brayman Hackel

Romeo and Juliet

Language and Writing

CATHERINE BELSEY

BLOOMSBURY

NEW DELHI • LONDON • OXFORD • NEW YORK • SYDNEY

BLOOMSBURY INDIA
Bloomsbury Publishing India Pvt. Ltd
Second Floor, LSC Building No. 4, DDA Complex, Pocket C–6&7,
Vasant Kunj, New Delhi 110070

BLOOMSBURY, BLOOMSBURY ACADEMIC INDIA and the Diana logo are trademarks of Bloomsbury Publishing Plc

First published in India 2023

This edition published with permission from Bloomsbury Publishing Plc,
50 Bedford Square, London, WC1B3DP, UK

British Library Cataloguing-in-Publication Data
A catalogue record for this book is available from the British Library

Library of Congress Cataloging-in-Publication Data
A catalog record for this book is available from the Library of Congress

ISBN: 978-93-94701-64-9

Typeset by Fakenham Prepress Solutions, Fakenham, Norfolk NR21 8NN
Printed and bound in India by Replika Press

To find out more about our authors and books
visit www.bloomsbury.com and sign up for our newsletters

CONTENTS

SERIES EDITOR'S PREFACE

This series puts the pedagogical expertise of distinguished literary critics at the disposal of students embarking upon Shakespeare Studies at university. While they demonstrate a variety of approaches to the plays, all the contributors to the series share a deep commitment to teaching and a wealth of knowledge about the culture and history of Shakespeare's England. The approach of each of the volumes is direct yet intellectually sophisticated and tackles the challenges Shakespeare presents. These volumes do not provide a shortcut to Shakespeare's works but instead offer a careful explication of them directed towards your own processing and interpretation of the plays and poems.

Students' needs in relation to Shakespeare revolve overwhelmingly around language, and Shakespeare's language is what most distinguishes him from his rivals and collaborators – as well as what most embeds him in his own historical moment. The *Language and Writing* series understands language as the very heart of Shakespeare's literary achievement rather than as an obstacle to be circumvented. This series addresses the difficulties often encountered in reading Shakespeare alongside the necessity of writing papers for university examinations and course assessment. The primary objective here is to foster rigorous critical engagement with the texts by helping you develop your own critical writing skills. *Language and Writing* titles demonstrate how to develop your own capacity to articulate and enlarge upon your experience of encountering the text, far beyond summarizing, paraphrasing or 'translating' Shakespeare's language into a more palatable, contemporary form. Each of the volumes in the series introduces the text as an act of specifically literary language and shows that the multifarious issues of life and history that Shakespeare's work addresses cannot be separated from their expression in language. In addition, each book takes you through a series of guidelines about how to develop viable undergraduate critical essays on the text in question, not by delivering interpretations but rather by taking you step-by-step through the process of discovering and developing your own critical ideas.

Each book includes chapters examining the text from the point of view of its composition, that is, from the perspective of Shakespeare's own process of composition as a reader, thinker and writer. The Introduction considers when and how the play was written, addressing, for example, the extant literary and cultural acts of language, from which Shakespeare constructed his work – including his sources – as well as the generic, literary and theatrical conventions at his disposal. Subsequent sections demonstrate how to engage in detailed examination and analysis of the text and focus on the literary, technical and historical intricacies of Shakespeare's verse and prose. Each volume also includes some discussion of performance. 'Language in Print' covers textual issues as well as the interpretation of the extant texts for any given play on stage and screen, treating, for example, the use of stage directions or parts of the play that are typically cut in performance. 'Language through Time' also addresses issues of stage/film history as they relate to the cultural evolution of Shakespeare's words. In addition, these chapters deal with the critical reception of the work, particularly the newer theoretical and historicist approaches that have revolutionized our understanding of Shakespeare's language over the last forty years. Crucially, every chapter contains a section on 'Writing Matters', which links the analysis of Shakespeare's language with your own critical writing.

The series empowers you to read and write about Shakespeare with scholarly confidence and will inspire your enthusiasm for doing so. The authors in this series have been selected because they combine scholarly distinction with outstanding teaching skills. Each book exposes the reader to an eminent scholar's teaching in action and expresses a vocational commitment to making Shakespeare accessible to a new generation of student readers.

Professor Dympna Callaghan
Series Editor
Arden Student Skills: Language and Writing

PREFACE

On the stage *Romeo and Juliet* gives immediate pleasure. Tender, passionate, funny, and sad in turn, the tragedy appeals to a wide range of audiences. Reflection on Shakespeare's language delivers more, however. To reopen in a succession of distinct contexts the questions the play raises is to reveal new possible readings. In this book I have reverted to some of the same issues under different headings, especially the way the play treats gender and genre, desire and violence, only to find that interpretation does not arrive at a single stopping point. New options continue to emerge from close attention to the words of the text and my project is to outline some of the choices available to us when we make sense of the play.

In the course of writing, I have incurred debts to Sandra Birnie, Christa Jansohn and Peter Roberts. John Astington advised on actors, Paul Werstine kindly put me straight on Chapter 5, while Alan Dessen has been generous in discussion of any and every aspect of the play. My gratitude to them all remains more rich in matter than in words.

CHAPTER ONE

Introduction: The play

Fatal love

Everyone knows the story of the doomed lovers. Romantic, lyrical, and forbidden to marry, they die for love, only to live on as icons of ideal passion. The play, just as immortal, it seems, has been filmed by George Cukor (1936), Franco Zeffirelli (1968) and, most notably, Baz Luhrmann in *William Shakespeare's Romeo + Juliet* (1996). It also remains recognizable in a range of generic transformations. The story was recreated as an opera in the eighteenth century by Georg Benda and in the nineteenth by Charles Gounod; it generated orchestral works by Berlioz (1839) and Tchaikovsky (1870) as well as a ballet by Sergei Prokofiev (1938). Adapted as a musical in *West Side Story* (1961), rewritten as the largely comic *Shakespeare in Love* (1998), converted to pornography in *Tromeo and Juliet* (1996) and horror in *Warm Bodies* (2013), the tale has remained in its various incarnations a blockbuster into our own times.

Juliet's name is a byword for love. I have just deleted an email message addressed to undisclosed recipients from a Miss Juliet, who wants to send me her photo. In Verona ('fair Verona, where we lay our scene') stands a life-size female figure in 'Juliet's house'. It is not exactly the golden statue promised at the end of the play, but made of bronze. Even so, since touching its breast brings luck in love, this part of the sculpture is highly polished and gleams in consequence almost like precious metal. Lovers also leave notes at 'Juliet's tomb' in the monastery of San Francesco al Corso to ask for her blessing, treating Shakespeare's fictional protagonist as one of love's saints.

Romeo, meanwhile, is virtually synonymous with *romantic lover*. Perhaps the first syllable of his name does half the work for him. 'Cards and flowers not enough for one Romeo', announced my local paper; the subject of this story had recruited a choir to serenade his girlfriend on Valentine's Day, it turned out. However, as Shakespeare's hero abandoned his first love without a backward glance in favour of Juliet, the name can also suggest a roving eye.

Even without having read it or seen it, many people feel familiar with this play. Most of us already know that the heroine declares her love at night on her balcony. Everyone can recite Juliet's 'wherefore art thou Romeo?' (2.2.33), although not everyone realizes that 'wherefore?' means 'why?'. The question already dwells, in its yearning, on the impossibility of their relationship. *Romeo and Juliet* is embedded in the fabric of Western culture and beyond. Although Shakespeare did not invent the story, his version gave its central figures a legendary place among lovers.

Its continuing stature means that it must be well worth our attention now. But why go back to Shakespeare himself? The play is over 400 years old, while the many reinscriptions, adaptations and redactions are designed precisely to bring it into the modern world. Why not settle for the modernizations instead? The answer, in my view, is that, when it comes to the language of love, no one does it better than Shakespeare. His version has entered into the vocabulary of romance and, perhaps at the same time, into our understanding of desire.

But that presents a problem for anyone confronted by the requirement to comment on the play. How can there be anything new to say about so influential a work? This book will propose that the language of the play reveals darker elements than the romantic legend acknowledges: the play has nearly as much to say about death as it has about love, and something to add about the links between the two. I shall also suggest that, when it comes to making sense of the text, there are choices to make, questions to resolve, and assumptions to challenge. Perhaps there is no such thing as the last word when it comes to interpretation, especially the interpretation of Shakespeare. There is always more to find, more to be said.

Authority and resistance

A tragedy is a play with an unhappy ending. The story of *Romeo and Juliet* certainly meets this requirement, moving with surprising speed from the excitement of falling in love to poison and bloodshed in the family vault. But there is another, contrary movement to be detected here, from the anarchic energy of the gang warfare in the opening scene to the ordered stillness of the golden statues. These 'statues' are tomb effigies (the word included both meanings at the time) and they are imagined as horizontal. Each set of parents will pay for the effigy of the other's child in solid gold, so that 'As rich shall Romeo by his lady's lie' (5.3.302). Shakespeare's audience might have thought of something like the elegant Italian-style effigies of Henry VII and Elizabeth of York in Westminster Abbey, already a tourist attraction at the time (http://blog.londonconnection.com/?p=2915).

There the king and queen are placed on their tomb, sheltered from time and change at the heart of a grand church. The rich figures of Romeo and Juliet will also belong on their monument in a church, designed to last for ever as emblems of reconciliation, although, as effigies, they will at the same time memorialize their tragic death as an effect of the feud. Already, the play is open to more than one interpretation, depending on whether we emphasize the sad story of the central figures, or the change their tale brings to the society that caused all the trouble.

And what sort of society is it? Wealthy, evidently, and perhaps extravagant: no expense is spared when Juliet's parents throw a party; anyone is welcome to attend, except their hereditary enemies. Romeo is a total stranger to the servant who, even so, blithely invites him too: 'My master is the great rich Capulet, and if you be not of the house of Montagues, I pray come and crush a cup of wine' (1.2.80–2). The society is hierarchic, as well: all the work seems to be done by servants; young men about town have apparently nothing to do except exchange puns, fall in love – and fight. Is there too much testosterone about and too little useful outlet for it? But above all, this is an autocratic world: a prince gives orders and expects obedience; parents believe they have the right to arrange their children's marriages.

As far as marriage is concerned, the Capulets start well enough. Juliet's father will not insist. His daughter is very young, and very dear to him, he tells her suitor; she is the only one of his children to have survived this long and he does not want any harm to come to her, especially in a world where childbirth is a dangerous process (1.2.8–14). On the other hand, if she is ready to marry, he is prepared to approve:

> But woo her, gentle Paris, get her heart.
> My will to her consent is but a part,
> And, she agreed, within her scope of choice
> Lies my consent and fair according voice. (1.2.15–18)

Lady Capulet initially broaches the matter with her daughter mildly, in the form of a question: 'Tell me, daughter Juliet, / How stands your dispositions to be married?' (1.3.65–6).

But these reasonable attitudes take for granted that Juliet will acquiesce in the wishes of her parents. 'I think', Capulet later assures Paris, 'she will be ruled / In all respects by me' (3.4.13–14). And almost at once supposition hardens into instruction. On Thursday, 'tell her', he instructs his wife, 'She shall be married to this noble earl' (20–1). So much for her consent.

The governor of this stratified and authoritarian society clearly has the best interests of his city at heart. Shakespeare's Prince, too, is an autocrat, if a benign one, and he makes very clear from the beginning that he won't stand for any more trouble: these feuds that disturb the peace have got to stop; if there are further outbreaks, the death penalty will be invoked (1.1.79–101). Capulet and Montague, he insists, must keep their people under control.

None of these assertions of authority has the desired effect. On the contrary, another fight breaks out and the consequence is the (tragic) banishment of Romeo; Juliet resists her father's instructions and the consequence is her (tragic) consignment to the Capulet tomb. It is not commands but their own understanding of what has happened that eventually brings the warring families to their senses. Perhaps, the play indicates, autocracy does not work; human beings are not always amenable to dictatorial methods of control; possibly there could be better ways of arranging social relations?

As it happens, at about this same time Shakespeare must have been writing a comedy that also challenged parental authority. *A Midsummer Night's Dream* concerns young people who reject a father's plans for his daughter's marriage. In this instance, the Duke eventually overrules the father to secure a happy ending. We cannot doubt that both plays invite theatregoers to align themselves with the young lovers against parental commands. How strange, we might reflect, that works more than four centuries old should display such modern sympathies. Shakespeare's own society was much more hierarchic than our own; although voices were raised in favour of marrying for love, aristocratic parents in the early modern world often expected in practice to choose their children's marriage partners. And yet here are works of fiction that show autocracy to be disastrous. Like *A Midsummer Night's Dream*, *Romeo and Juliet* supports values in advance of its own society, and perhaps identifies an element in its culture that points forward towards our own.

Consent as a condition of good social relations could not be taken for granted in the early modern word. Indeed, it cannot always be relied on even now. Fiction, then, it seems, does not have to confine itself to mirroring the way things are. Instead, it can imagine how they might be, and measure the reality outside the theatre against that imagined state of affairs. Comedy (sometimes) dreams of a better world and dramatizes that dream; tragedy (sometimes) throws into relief the limitations of the existing one, showing how far it falls short of the ideal.

Shakespeare's stagecraft

It is always a good idea to see the play – on the stage if possible but, failing that, on film. Seeing the whole tragedy at a sitting gives a good idea of its architecture, the structure of the action that so easily gets lost in the detailed process of reading. A good production can bring out Shakespeare's storytelling skills, still unsurpassed, some would say. After the Prologue (and there will be more to say about that shortly), the play proper opens with two servants spoiling for a fight.

I once saw *A Midsummer Night's Dream* in a theatre that turned out to be full of schoolchildren. My heart sank as I anticipated the rustling sweet packets and catcalls that were bound to distract my attention from the action on the stage. But the director was ahead of me. The curtain rose on an unscripted martial arts encounter between Theseus and the Amazon Hippolyta. A respectful silence descended in the auditorium and was broken only when the time came to register an intelligent appreciation of the comic antics to follow.

Shakespeare's Globe was a busy, noisy place. Nothing, however, commands initial audience attention better than a fight. What in the reading of the opening scene of *Romeo and Juliet* is as flat as a pancake – a series of laboured and now virtually impenetrable puns – can be electrifying in its menace if it is well done, especially as it builds up to a full-scale brawl. Baz Luhrmann's *William Shakespeare's Romeo + Juliet* wonderfully captures the frenetic energy of the encounter, very little of it evident on the page in the laconic stage direction, *They fight.*

What is more, the main impediment to a happy outcome of the love story is established in the process. Even the servants of the two opposing families are at each other's throats, and for no apparent reason, except that they just hate each other. Was there ever a cause for this feud? If so, it is evidently lost in the mists of time, but the venom is no less intense for that. Benvolio, whose name means 'good will' in Italian, is unable to part the contestants, even when he invokes the words of Jesus from the cross as he asked God to forgive his killers, 'you know not what you do' (1.1.63, Luke 23.34). Tybalt's part is already sharply defined here in his remorseless contempt for Benvolio's appeal for peace: 'I hate the word / As I hate hell, all Montagues, and thee' (1.1.68–9). Nameless citizens materialize, eager to take sides in what has become open war, and then the principals declare themselves ready to join in. Old Capulet in his dressing gown calls for a sword, despite his wife's reminder that a crutch would suit his age better, and while he lays hands on old Montague, only the entrance of the Prince puts a stop to the senseless violence by naming the penalty that will in due course have the effect of parting the lovers.

Act 1 keeps us waiting and guessing. Not until the context has been vividly established in this way does the play turn its attention to the hero. Romeo is a puzzle: he is keeping himself to himself, seeking solitude, shunning his friends, sad. What can be the cause, his family wonder. Knowing the story in advance, as modern playgoers do, and as many in Shakespeare's first audiences would have done, spectators might think they know. He is in love – with Juliet, obviously

– and the relationship is doomed for the reason we have just witnessed. The clue, after all, is presumably in the title. But that guess would be wrong. The drama plays with expectations when it withholds the name of the woman he loves, until Romeo himself comes across it by chance in a list of guests to be invited to the Capulet dinner: 'Rosaline'. Rosaline? *Romeo and Rosaline*? Surely not!

Tom Stoppard's screenplay for *Shakespeare in Love* toys briefly with that possibility, before reverting to Henslowe's preferred name, *Romeo and Ethel the Pirate's Daughter*. 'Good title', the producer comments reflectively, calculating the likely income from ticket sales; the fictional Christopher Marlowe, however, rolls his eyes. In actuality, of course, there was never any doubt: Shakespeare's main source was Arthur Brooke's translation of an Italian story, published in English as *The Tragical History of Romeus and Juliet*.

The unfolding plot builds suspense and tension. Once the feud has been established and the hero invested with enigma, 1.3 at last brings us to the heroine named in the title, but not before Paris has been invited to the Capulet feast to woo her, while Romeo has determined to gatecrash the same party in order to see Rosaline. And how does the play give Juliet her own history and context? By means of her garrulous Nurse, with only four teeth left, mother to a dead daughter whose birth qualified her to breastfeed Juliet, effectively a surrogate mother to Juliet herself, and source of a salacious interest in anything connected, however tenuously, with sex.

If the Nurse offers the audience a different perspective on love from the elaborate poetic conceits of Romeo in 1.1, Mercutio provides yet another, this time sceptical, and only after that do the protagonists meet and fall romantically in love at first sight. But ominously, the feud resurfaces when Tybalt spots a Montague at the Capulet feast, while the lovers discover, independently, each other's last names. All the main pieces are now in place. 'O dear account!' (there will be a high price to pay for this), exclaims Romeo, with a pun on 'dear': his new love is both precious to him and metaphorically expensive. 'My life is my foe's debt' (my life is mortgaged to my enemy; 1.5.117). 'My only love sprung from my only hate', laments Juliet (1.5.137), indicating that she too understands the implications of their position.

By the end of the first act of the play, then, the main figures are vividly before us, and the obstacles they face are clear. When later novelists move our attention from one set of characters to another, gradually revealing how the groups are interlocked in the plot, or when modern film directors plunge us into the action, before unfolding what the alignments defined there will mean for the characters, they have learnt their storytelling skills directly or indirectly from Shakespeare's stagecraft.

The language of the time

If it is good to see the play, it is also good to read it. Shakespeare's language can be a deterrent to the faint-hearted but it repays the attention reading permits. And it is well worth coming to terms with. Understand the language and command the power to make your own independent interpretation; try to ignore it, or rely on the paraphrase of others, and remain forever at the mercy of other people's readings. Like any language, Shakespeare's gets easier with practice.

In the first instance, a number of archaisms from four centuries ago now survive, if at all, mainly in poetry, testifying in the process to Shakespeare's influence on the subsequent tradition. In 3.5 alone, *ere* (before), *bark* (ship; a vestige of the term remains in *embark*), *flood* (sea, river), *hurdle* (bier). On the stage such words barely delay us: playgoers get the sense, even if a word or two remains unfamiliar; on the page they can be alienating. Moreover, it is easy to be put off by the *thees* and *thous*. The distinction between *thou* and *you* has disappeared from modern English but in the Middle Ages it mattered, much as the difference between *tu* and *vous* does in French. *You* was formal, respectful, or plural: *thou* was singular, intimate, used in prayer, and a way of addressing social inferiors. Shakespeare's moment was transitional and the distinctions do not hold consistently: in the play friends and relations may be *you* or *thou*, apparently indiscriminately. But it is notable that the dialogue between Romeo and Juliet in the orchard is conducted entirely in the intimate form: indeed, each addresses the other as *thou* even in soliloquy (2.2.26, 33). In that respect, an early modern audience might well have registered, as we generally do not, a switch of pronouns in their very first exchange. Juliet politely calls this stranger 'you' (1.5.96) but within a few lines Romeo replies with 'thou' (103). Is he, perhaps, taking advantage of the conceit that he is praying to a saint in order to adopt the privilege of a lover?

Thanks to the transition between medieval and modern English, and because most editions give Shakespeare in familiar modern spelling, there are also a number of false friends for modern readers to reckon with. *An* can mean *if*: 'an we be in choler, we'll draw' (that is, *if* we're angry, we'll draw our swords, 1.1.3); *a* (or *a'*, or *'a*, depending on the modern editor's preference) can mean *on*: 'A' Thursday let it be, a' Thursday, tell her' (3.4.20), or sometimes *he* 'An 'a speak anything against me I'll take him down, an 'a were lustier than he is', says the Nurse, aware that the lusty (energetic, vigorous) Mercutio has been teasing her, but not entirely sure how (2.4.144–5). Meanwhile, *but* can mean *only*: 'Speak but one rhyme and I am satisfied' (2.1.9), 'An but thou love me, let them find me here', Romeo exclaims, affirming that if only Juliet loves him, he is willing to risk death at the hands of her kinsmen (2.2.76).

Most of those details are a matter of indifference on the stage, but some elements of vocabulary have changed enough to be potentially misleading. *Gentle* embraces a much wider range of meanings in early modern usage than it does now. To be *gentle* was to be of noble birth (as in *gentleman*, *gentlewoman*), a condition that was supposed to bring with it courtesy and considerateness. To call someone *gentle* was to flatter their status and their good behaviour: 'Content thee, gentle coz', says Capulet (1.5.64), in the hope of soothing the fiery Tybalt, who has just threatened to kill Romeo and is anything but *gentle* in our sense. *Sad* can mean *serious*, as well as *sad*: Benvolio asks Romeo, 'Tell me in sadness, who is that you love' (be serious; stop playing with words) and Romeo replies (still playing with words and invoking the modern meaning of sadness), 'What, shall I groan and tell thee?' 'In sadness, cousin, I do love a woman' (1.1.197–202). Much of this is more confusing in the telling than in hearing or reading the text. The best way to learn Shakespeare's English is to become immersed in it, so that strange usages grow familiar.

Perhaps all moments are transitional when it comes to language, which alters continuously. Even so, early modern English was growing and changing at a special pace. The vernacular was in the process of replacing Latin as a means of learned exchange and acquiring a new confidence in the process, as well as a vastly increased range. Probably first performed in 1595, *Romeo and Juliet* must have been written when the playwright was about thirty. His later works would be more austere, more economical with words at key points; this one, by contrast, revels in the developing possibilities of the English language.

Copiousness

Words are the primary material of the writer's craft, and awareness of what they can do makes the difference that defines a well-told story, a good joke, or a clever song. And to that extent words are material in another sense of that term: substantial, not transparent, not offered merely as access to some imagined message on the other side of language. Language can itself be a source of pleasure in inventiveness, ingenuity. Never, the young Shakespeare's own prescription might have been, use three words where ten will do. The recipe he follows is probably the exact opposite of the one the critic should obey, but the copiousness of the language, at first an obstacle to comprehension, turns out in due course to be a rich source of meanings that expand on and refine the simple tale we know.

Romeo's account of daybreak offers an incidental example. The newly-weds have spent the night together and now they must part: Romeo has been banished from Verona on pain of death; if he is seen, he will risk execution. Surely it cannot be morning already, Juliet protests. Romeo, just as reluctant to leave, knows better:

> Look, love, what envious streaks
> Do lace the severing clouds in yonder east.
> Night's candles are burnt out, and jocund day
> Stands tiptoe on the misty mountain tops. (3.5.7–10)

There must be a quicker way to make the point: 'look at the clock'; 'it's getting light'. What, then, does the play gain by protracting the moment?

In the first instance, delay itself. The lyrical exchanges literally prolong the time the lovers spend together – and the time the audience has to immerse itself in the romance. In the second place, the dialogue dwells on the complex mixture of feelings involved. The text does more than ask us to imagine ourselves in the situation of the lovers on the assumption that we already know what it would be like: it puts before playgoers, in what they hear as well as what they see, the specificity of parting in such circumstances. This scene of separation adds nothing much to the plot: instead, it enlists the audience in sharing the feelings of the lovers by slowing down the action and focusing on their emotions.

'Look, love ...' Romeo is contradicting his bride, but in the most affectionate way. 'Look, love, what envious streaks / Do lace the severing clouds in yonder east'. The dawn is parting the dark masses in the sky, just as it must part the night-time lovers. Most commentators read 'lace' as decorative: the sky is now marked with patches of gold and silver embroidery. But there is an additional option, more pointed in the context. The 'streaks' of light that separate the clouds resemble to Romeo's eyes the laces that criss-cross Elizabethan bodices: dawn is lacing up the sky, ready for its daytime visibility. Juliet, we assume, fresh from their shared bed, is still in her shift or nightgown, but in the daytime she will be laced into her dress and returned to the proprieties she owes to the public gaze. It is as if Romeo foresees what must happen in his absence, perceiving an anticipation in the dawn sky of Juliet putting on her clothes. The 'envious' light of morning jealously ends the private intensity of the lovers' night of passion.

'Night's candles are burnt out.' This reference, for us slightly exotic, would have been ordinary for Shakespeare's original audience, who lit their homes with candles as a matter of course. The candles have burned down and guttered out, and with them the sexual encounter imaged, perhaps, in their flames. But Romeo, who evidently gestures towards 'yonder east', is looking at the sky, so that the candles in question are also the stars, pinpoints of brightness that pale to nothing in the light of dawn. 'And jocund day / Stands tiptoe on the misty mountaintops.' The morning is cheerful, smiling, even playful. Careless of the lovers, the day personified stands on tiptoe, partly in order to peer over the tops of the mountains that mask the rising sun, and partly because it is eager to pursue its own job of lighting up the whole sky. Outside the circle of their embrace, life goes on, indifferent to the relationship between two individuals.

The passage is poetic, lyrical, and highly inventive, but its details are familiar to the audience: laces, candles, standing on tiptoe. Its vocabulary, in other words, is everyday. By this means the play invites the audience to feel with and for its central figures as if they were real. That *as if* is important too: real people do not, and almost certainly never did, talk in iambic pentameters, even if those lines are broken up, as here, to mimic speech. Fiction, or Shakespeare's fiction at any rate, is not merely lifelike. There will be more to say about this in due course.

Writing matters

There is always more to say about the relationship between fiction and the world, but there's no time like the present, so we might begin to think about it now. And there's no better way than writing to discover what you think. If reading Shakespeare well demands concentration, writing well about Shakespeare requires confidence. And confidence comes with practice. The best way forward is to start writing at once, but a full-scale essay under the rubric 'Discuss' might not be the ideal place to start. Meanwhile, other people's ideas in casebooks and anthologies may look like a lifeline but actually only defer the moment of direct engagement with the text.

So how about beginning, instead, with the text itself? We can afford to start small – with the Prologue. The joy of computers is that even single paragraphs can be assembled gradually and kept for future use. A growing savings bank of written insights wonderfully boosts morale. Even before reading or seeing the play, it is possible to analyze these 14 lines spoken by the Chorus, and in the process develop the skills that foster an individual sense of how Shakespeare's words work.

A number of questions could usefully be addressed, first among them, what kind of play is it that *has* a Prologue, and one delivered in verse at that? We are so accustomed to seeing on television and at the cinema fiction that claims to mimic what we think of as real life, that it is easy to miss how far the project of Shakespeare's plays differs from that current model. In fact, after a century of modernist experiment on the stage, we ought to be aware that there are other modes of drama. Luigi Pirandello, Bertholt Brecht, Samuel Beckett and Harold Pinter, among others, have variously broken with 'realism', and not least because for different reasons they regard it as a form of illusionism: 'realism' sets out to create the illusion that what the spectator sees is *really* happening before our very eyes. The term *illusionism* also implies what we already know if we pause to think about it, that this is achieved by a conjuring trick, or at least a succession of strategies for involving the audience in the construction of an illusory reality. We are aware, of course, that we are watching a work of fiction, that the events are carefully staged to resemble actuality, and may be created by what we admire as 'special effects', but we expect to be coaxed to suspend, as Samuel Taylor Coleridge puts it, our disbelief.

Despite the best efforts of modernist writers to lure us out of our comfort zone, 'realism' (aka illusionism) remains the default position. This is the mode of most Hollywood cinema, soap opera, situation comedy, and television series. And these genres do not generally entail prologues. On occasions when they have recourse to voiceover to introduce the story, the tone is generally low-key, not poetic, but as conversational as the majority of the dialogue. Such 'realism' rules out any mention within the work of the work itself as a fiction staged for the benefit of observers.

Shakespeare's Prologue, by contrast, betrays no such inhibitions. It brazenly acknowledges that it is spoken on behalf of the cast and crew; it admits to creating a setting, 'Verona, where we lay our scene' (l. 2), and then goes on to call the play 'the two hours' traffic of our stage' (l. 12). Moreover, in the process, surprisingly enough, this acknowledgement deprecates the work of the dramatist himself. 'Traffic' is in the first instance trade, the exchange of goods, merchandise, and the travelling involved in conducting trade. Such activity is mundane, quotidian, a world away from the heroic grandeur we rightly associate with tragedy in general, and Shakespeare in particular.

How far is the Prologue a part of the play? At once inside and outside the work itself, not contributing to the action, and yet written for an actor to perform, the Prologue is evidently entitled to comment, however ironically, on the quality of the play itself. And it foregrounds the work of the performers. The play itself may not be much, the Prologue indicates, but we shall do our best with this modest material: 'What here shall miss, our toil shall strive to mend' (14). Clearly, this is a form of theatre that relishes its own status as fiction, and implicitly invites applause for the art of acting. If the writer's skills are defective (and the proof or disproof of that pudding will be in what follows), perhaps the performance will make up for any failings.

Baz Luhrmann, modernizing what he calls, not without irony of his own, *William Shakepeare's Romeo + Juliet*, inventively gives the Prologue a 'realistic' treatment, when he turns it into a TV news bulletin, read in the brisk, neutral, dispassionate voice of a newscaster. There is an excellent case for this way of presenting it: a great deal of information is packed into Shakespeare's 14 lines, in the same way as news condenses the tears and tantrums of events into bullet-point accounts that extract the essentials from a mass of circumstantial detail. In the first instance, an account of the Prologue might attend to this condensation. How much information does it deliver, and in what order? A good news bulletin would tell us who does what, where, and what the consequences are. How does Shakespeare's bulletin measure up?

But the film is not satisfied that its initial treatment does justice to the Prologue, and a sonorous voice repeats the first six lines more slowly and audibly. Evidently, the assumption is that there is something here worth hearing. *Shakespeare in Love*, meanwhile, adds backstage drama to the moment by allotting the Prologue to a stammerer. Will he be able to get through it without stuttering? But, after a shaky start, he gathers speed, speaking clearly and with mounting confidence, miraculously confirming Henslowe's insistence that everything will turn out well, even though no one knows how or why. And as he speaks, the audience in the Globe, inclined at first to snigger, settles down, hushed and attentive.

Are there features of the text of the Prologue that justify this audience response? First, it tells a story, with a beginning, middle and an end. And second, it recounts the tale in a vocabulary that, as usual in Shakespeare, embraces more than at first glance meets the eye. 'Two households' (1). What does the word imply? As 1.1 will confirm, the feud is not purely personal: it constrains all members of each household from the head of the house to the servants. Moreover, households at this time represent lineages, the powerful names of Capulet and Montague, transmitted down the generations, that will dominate the action and burden the young lovers with a heritage they cannot simply ignore or cast aside. That the houses are 'both alike in dignity' implies not only equal status, equal grandeur, but also the improbability that one will ever prevail over the other. The feud is not likely to be ended by one side winning.

Now it is your turn. What do you make of the antithesis between 'ancient' and 'new' in l. 3? How does 'grudge' differ from 'mutiny'? And what point is made by the repetition of 'civil' and 'civil' in l. 4? *Civil* can mean *of the city or community* (as in *civil society*), *internal to that community* (as in *civil war*), and *proper, well-conducted, polite* (as in *civilized*). How many of those meanings are in play in Shakespeare's pun? What can we say about 'fatal loins' (l. 5)? Doesn't that phrase, in the first instance, formulate a contradiction (it is technically an oxymoron)? Loins give life, but in this case they also bring death, as a result of the two distinct lineages at war. Etymologically, 'fatal' aligns itself with fate and, at the same time, 'loins' move us effortlessly into the realm of sexuality, anticipating the new topic of the 'star-crossed lovers' (l. 6). That last phrase has become proverbial, but what does it mean here? From the fatal loins of their distinct families, the lovers 'take their life' (l. 6). Given that they are already fated, star-crossed, do they come to life in this phrase, or kill themselves?

How much of the density and complexity of the language would playgoers have picked up? After all, we have to disentangle it over time and with an effort. It is possible that Shakespeare's original audience, or parts of it, would have taken in more than we do. In the first place, the language was not archaic to them. And in the second, Elizabethans were probably more accustomed to listening than we are. The Prologue asks for 'patient ears'. Early modern audiences went to 'hear' a play as often as they went to see one.

I don't pretend to have exhausted the possibilities of the meanings inscribed in the Prologue. Equip yourself with the tools of the trade, in particular a good edition with explanatory notes, but also a dictionary that includes usages which have become obsolete. The full Oxford English Dictionary, available online or in print in university libraries, not only offers historical definitions but provides quotations showing the range of nuances available in earlier epochs. This means extra work but it allows much more insight into the subtlety of Shakespeare's usages than one-word glosses that offer to 'translate' his vocabulary.

Before we abandon the Prologue, a word on structure. The speech is a sonnet, a poetic form in vogue in the 1590s, when the play was first performed. Sonnets are generally about love, and are usually addressed to the beloved. The appropriation of the genre for narrative brings together the main features of the tragedy as a *story* about *love*. This is a characteristic Shakespearean sonnet: 14 lines, divided into three sets of four lines (quatrains) and a rhyming couplet. Each of the first two quatrains ends in a full stop, packaging a distinct part of the tale. It would be worth thinking about how narrative is divided. The third quatrain acknowledges that it *is* a tale, and the couplet appeals to the audience for patient attention. That patient attention is exactly what we shall need if we are to do justice to Shakespeare's remarkable play.

And in case you feel you want still more to say about the Prologue, there is an old trick well known to critics, which involves bringing the text into relation to another that resembles it in some way. The point is to focus on the differences. (Difference is the life-blood of criticism and, indeed, some would say, of thinking itself.) Shakespeare did not invent the prefatory sonnet: the model was there in the main source, Arthur Brooke's *Romeus and Juliet*. I include Brooke's poem here without comment for comparison and contrast with Shakespeare's. What does Shakespeare's do that Brooke's doesn't (and, if you like, vice versa)? More important from the point of view of audience suspense, what does Shakespeare's *not* do?

Love hath inflamed twain by sudden sight
    And both do grant the thing that both desire.
    They wed in shrift by counsel of a friar.
    Young Romeus climbs fair Juliet's bower by night.
Three months he doth enjoy his chief delight.
    By Tybalt's rage provoked unto ire,
    He payeth death to Tybalt for his hire.
    A banished man, he scapes by secret flight.
New marriage is offered to his wife.
    She drinks a drink that seems to reave her breath:
    They bury her, that sleeping yet hath life.
Her husband hears the tidings of her death.
    He drinks his bane. And she with Romeus' knife,
When she awakes, herself, alas! she slay'th.

reave: take away
bane: poison

Reading matters too

Once you've filed your views on the Prologue, the next task is to read the play: the play, note, not critics, not even this book. Critics can do their best to make the play come alive for you; they can on occasions come up with information and ideas that you might not have thought of; some of us can even do our best to entertain you; but what no one can do for you is read the text.

And that has to be the starting point. It is much easier to come up with ideas of your own if your head is not already full of other people's. See what *you* think. You can modify and refine it later, if you find yourself persuaded by arguments, but confidence comes from knowing that you have thoughts worth thinking.

You do.

CHAPTER TWO

The language of love

Torches

Love idealizes the object of desire. As the young people dance and the old men gossip at the Capulet feast, Romeo first sets eyes on Juliet. Who is the lady partnering that knight, he asks a passing servant, but the man does not know. 'O', exclaims Romeo, 'she doth teach the torches to burn bright.' And he continues, 'It seems she hangs upon the cheek of night / As some rich jewel in an Ethiop's ear, / Beauty too rich for use, for earth too dear' (1.5.43–6).

Juliet's beauty exceeds the light of the torches. In the hall that the audience is invited to imagine as the setting for the event, candles would not have provided the only illumination. 'More light', demands Capulet, anxious to ensure a resplendent occasion (1.5.27). Torches were rods or poles with flammable material attached at the top. They were carried at night by travellers making their way through the unlit streets: when his guests leave, Capulet calls for 'More torches here!' (1.5.124). Later, Juliet will choose to see the dawn as a flaming meteor designed to act as a torchbearer, lighting Romeo's way to Mantua (3.5.12–15). Paris will urge his boy to put out the torch at the tomb, in order to avoid drawing attention to his presence (5.3.1–2), while Romeo's torch alerts Paris himself to the arrival of a newcomer (21). Indoors, torches might be placed in sconces or brackets attached to the walls; alternatively, they might be held by servants, or perhaps by the partygoers themselves. Before the feast Romeo has already made great play of his role as torchbearer: he is too much in love to dance, he insists; he will hold a torch instead and watch from the sidelines (1.4.11; 35–8).

The drama has a motive for repeatedly alluding to these lighting effects. Darkness was not an option in the public theatres, where plays were performed in the open air in the afternoons. Playgoers, like readers, are asked to imagine a succession of night-time scenes. Among them, the feast itself is brilliantly illuminated, we are to suppose, with a view to showing that no expense has been spared in this display of hospitality and wealth – the first, perhaps, a mark of the second.

In Romeo's eyes Juliet teaches the torches to burn bright; she sets an example for their flames to aspire to, showing them what true radiance looks like. (My clumsy paraphrase throws into relief the eloquence of the line itself.) She stands out from the surrounding darkness, Romeo goes on, like a precious earring glittering against a black cheek, 'Beauty too rich for use, for earth too dear' (1.5.46). And now Romeo is eager to touch her hand, if still not to dance (50).

How does this instant access of idealizing passion compare with his love for Rosaline, which led him to walk in the woods at night and shut himself in his room all day with the blinds down (1.1.129–38)? The misery of Rosaline's rejection renders Romeo antisocial but for his friend Benvolio he makes an effort: 'Where shall we dine? O me! What fray was here?' (1.1.171). But he doesn't really want to know: 'Yet tell me not, for I have heard it all' (172). The little he reveals to Benvolio defines the previous emotion mainly in a series of elaborate conceits:

> Love is a smoke made with the fume of sighs;
> Being purged, a fire sparkling in lover's eyes;
> Being vexed, a sea nourished with loving tears.

What is it else? A madness most discreet,
A choking gall, and a preserving sweet. (1.1.188–92)

Conceits complicate an account, perhaps lifting it above the ordinary, avoiding cliché, or just drawing attention to their own inventiveness. I can't help thinking that the early modern audience would have to work at this nearly as hard as we do. But not quite. They might have recognized that a line each is allotted to three of the four elements in play here: air (sighs), fire, and water (tears). Evidently, there is nothing of the fourth, earth, in this passion. They would also have relished the piling of one paradox on another: a sensible madness, a poison that kills and at the same time gives life with its sweetness. The role model for Elizabethan love poets was Petrarch, whose sonnets to Laura explored the contradictions of love as a state that both burns and freezes, a delightful sadness, a desire that only increases as it is expended. 'Now', comments Mercutio, as Romeo appears, 'is he for the numbers that Petrarch flowed in', adding for good hyperbolic measure, 'Laura to his lady was a kitchen wench' (2.4.38–40).

It would be easy to suppose that a love formulated with such indulgence is not genuine, that Romeo is more in love with love, as they say, or even with language itself, than with Rosaline. The Friar will in due course accuse him of 'doting', not loving (2.3.78). But Romeo counters by pointing out that this love was unrequited (81–3); Rosaline was indifferent to Romeo's attentions, as was Laura to Petrarch's. And what else do lovers do in such circumstances but read poems, listen to love songs, write novels, or think and talk obsessively about their condition? The signifier in the form of words, phrases, images, tunes, stories, stands in for the desired relationship and, while it does so, goes some way to defer the pain. 'Thy love did read by rote', insists the Friar (84). But love, even true love, we know, prompts poetry. Moreover, Juliet herself is not above a Petrarchan paradox: 'Parting is such sweet sorrow' (2.2.184); 'The more I give to thee, / The more I have' (2.2.134–5); loss is gain: 'learn me how to lose a winning match, / Played for a pair of stainless maidenhoods' (3.2.12–13).

In the view that Romeo's love for Rosaline was not real, I perceive a residue of the belief, characteristic of Victorian fiction, that there is for each of us only one true love. Perhaps Shakespeare, like the twenty-first century, is less innocent, or more realistic, recognizing that each successive new love always seems to be the genuine one. 'Did my heart love till now? Forswear it, sight. / For I ne'er saw true beauty till this night' (1.5.51–2). Or is the Friar right in one way? Is a hopelessly one-sided love always folly, infatuation, 'doting', confined as it mostly is to fantasy, and thus in the first instance to the signifier, to creativity with images, or music, to playing with words? *Romeo and Juliet* keeps its options open when it comes to the value of Romeo's first love.

In love with Juliet, Romeo becomes altogether more active, more heroic, leaping orchard walls and risking death in the process. If Romeo is now energetic, less inclined to mope, that may be, as he says, because his new love does not reject him. And here, too, there is already wordplay, even if this is less evident on the surface and not necessarily deliberate on Romeo's part. When at first sight he describes Juliet's beauty as 'too rich for use, for earth too dear' (1.5.46), the meaning is apparently obvious: it is too precious for everyday wear, too special for this earth. So indeed it will prove: there will be no ordinary life in the everyday world for these lovers. Although he does not know it, Romeo's praise foreshadows the tragic ending – and appeals to the superior knowingness of playgoers familiar with the story.

At the same time, however, 'use' also means usury, loan that attracts interest. Juliet's beauty is too valuable to be lent out, and therefore, we might think to ourselves, too rare to be conferred, as her parents wish, on the highest bidder. Sometimes characters tell the audience more than they themselves know.

'Earth', meanwhile, can also mean the grave, as it does when Capulet tells Paris, as he does in most editions (although not in Arden 3), 'Earth hath swallowed all my hopes but she' (1.2.14; cf. 3.2.59). 'The earth that's nature's mother is her tomb', Friar Laurence observes sententiously (2.3.5). In that light Romeo's praise perhaps incorporates a meaning that is the opposite of the obvious one: Juliet's beauty, 'for earth too dear', might be understood as too perfect to be subject to death. Knowing the story, as we do but Romeo does not, are we entitled to perceive more than he realizes in the lover's assertion that his lady is too beautiful to be mortal? If so, it is one that will return as a full-scale dramatic irony in the tomb of the Capulets, when Romeo sees Juliet, now consigned to earth and, as he mistakenly supposes, dead, and yet unaccountably still 'fair' (5.3.102). She is indeed at this moment too fair to be a corpse. While the audience vainly wills him not to miss this clue, Romeo's phrasing recapitulates in that gloomy setting his opening comparison with the torches: 'here lies Juliet, and her beauty makes / This vault a feasting presence full of light' (85–6).

Gender and sex

Romeo has not given up on conceits now that he has found Juliet. In the orchard, he sees her appear above: 'But soft, what light through yonder window breaks? / It is the east and Juliet is the sun!' (2.2.2–3). These lines are hard to resist, until they are followed by an elaborate fable about the envy directed to this sun by her maid, the moon, personified as Diana, goddess of chastity. The moon is pale from green-sickness, the anaemia once thought to afflict young women while they remained virgins (4–9; cf. 3.5.156). The relevance of this story to Romeo's situation is not immediately apparent, but in due course we reach the point: the pallor of 'vestal' virgins is folly. There is a complicated pun here: 'vestal' virgins were Roman priestesses sworn to celibacy; 'vest-al livery' is what virgins wear, at once pale skin and fools' coats. Romeo appeals to the moon to 'Cast it [virginity] off' (9). However idealized his passion might be, it is evidently directed squarely at sex.

Modern directors often cut such passages in performance, and perhaps we just have to recognize that Elizabethan tastes ran to such elaborations. On the other hand, this represents an instance of the copiousness characteristic of early Shakespeare. Later, he would become more economical: possibly, sixteenth-century tastes were not, after all, so different from our own in this respect.

If Romeo knows what he wants, so, it seems, does Juliet, and this might constitute more of a surprise to our own contemporaries, all too ready to assume that virtuous young women were culturally required to be demure and coy, until twentieth-century feminism rode to the rescue of female desire. Cultural history, it seems, is not quite so straightforward: in her history of popular romance Helen Cooper demonstrates that earlier heroines often initiated the process of falling in love; it was not until a later century that virtuous young women were expected to be less interested in sex than men were.

Ann Radcliffe's Gothic mystery *The Italian* was published in 1797, coincidentally 200 years after the first printed version of *Romeo and Juliet*. The novel copies the scene at Juliet's window, but with a striking difference. In the opening chapter the hero defies his family's prohibition to make his way by night into the garden of the woman he loves. Hearing her sigh at her window and then pronounce his name, he reveals his presence. His beloved's response is very different from Juliet's: 'She stood fixed for an instant, while her countenance changed to an ashy paleness; and then, with trembling haste closing the lattice, quitted the apartment', not to return.

This, too, is love, but in the eighteenth-century text propriety is stronger than passion. Juliet, by contrast, takes a positive role in the courtship process. She, too, sighs at her window; she speaks her lover's name. But she goes much further than her intertextual descendent: 'Romeo, doff thy name, / And for thy name, which is no part of thee, / Take all myself' (2.2.47–9). The rest of the scene will make clear that this taking of her whole self is to occur within the legitimate bonds of marriage, but already we know that now there is no going back. At this moment, Romeo steps forward: 'I take thee at thy word' (49). By implication, this reciprocal *taking* anticipates the wedding ceremony, which we do not see. And while it seems that the contract in the orchard effectively represents the moment when *I, Romeo, take thee Juliet*, the play overturns the order given in the Book of Common Prayer: it is the woman who speaks first.

In *The Origins of Sex* Faramerz Dabhoiwala traces the transition that takes place in the course of the Enlightenment. Until the seventeenth century it was generally assumed that women were equally capable of desire and sexual pleasure; by 1800, however, it was just as widely believed that men were the lustful and predatory sex, while women, or at least good women, were expected to act as a restraining force. Dabhoiwala's sources are not predominantly literary, or for the earlier period he might have brought in evidence the myth of Tiresias, no doubt familiar from Ovid's *Metamorphoses* to products of the Tudor grammar schools. Asked to resolve the question of relative enjoyment, Tiresias, who had been both man and woman, declared that women's pleasure in love was greater than men's.

Juliet, then, is by no means out of line with her culture. She does not turn pale or retreat from the window. Instead, her first thoughts are for Romeo's safety in the light of her family's hostility to his: 'If they do see thee, they will murder thee' (1. 70), and for what this would mean to her: 'I would not for the world they saw thee here' (74). Only then does she reflect on the proprieties: women are supposed to play hard to get. Juliet knows what convention requires: the harsh and indifferent mistress of Elizabethan lyric poetry puts her lover through many trials and tribulations before she yields to his advances.

The 'cruel fair' of the Petrarchan poet's desire had no need to spell out her reasons, so deeply held in the culture that they went without saying. In the first place, virginity was precious. Marriage among the wealthy was above all a matter of dynasty and property. Old Capulet is proud to have found his daughter a potential husband 'of noble parentage' first, and next 'Of fair demesnes [lands]'. Paris is 'nobly ligned' (aligned, socially related, or of noble lineage, with an additional aural pun on 'lined', or well-heeled, as we might say). Not until after that does Capulet reach his honourable character and handsome proportions (3.5.180–3). Where descent is the main issue, the chastity of the bride is of the highest importance: in a world without effective contraception or blood tests, the sole guarantee a man had of paternity was thought to be the virginity of his bride and her absolute fidelity thereafter as a wife. Even so, Shakespeare's plays are full of jokes about having only the mother's word for the legitimacy of the child.

Young women, however much in love they might be, were well advised to hold off until they could be sure of their suitors' intentions. Virginity, once lost, was not replaceable; the woman who had yielded to impulse became damaged goods in the marriage market. Moreover, to give in easily was to invite contempt. In addition, courtship represented the one time in a patriarchal society when the woman held the reins. For this moment, she was the centre of attention, the recipient of gifts and praise, since she had the power to concede or refuse. Parents could cajole and threaten but, even if consent was given under duress, the church consistently treated the willingness of the bride as a condition of marriage. It was therefore in the woman's interests to prolong the moment of her supremacy for as long as possible. Juliet has unwittingly given the game away. And yet perhaps she could pretend, if it would sustain Romeo's addresses:

> if thou think'st I am too quickly won,
> I'll frown and be perverse and say thee nay,
> So thou wilt woo, but else not for the world. (2.2.95–7)

It is too late to retreat, however, and Juliet is anxious to reassure Romeo that her readiness to reciprocate his love does not imply a lightness in her affections: 'trust me, gentleman, I'll prove more true / Than those that have more cunning to be strange' (100–1).

Her love, she tells Romeo, is 'as boundless as the sea' (133). His is also insatiable: 'O, wilt thou leave me so unsatisfied?' he demands (125), as she says goodnight. The exact reference of that line is probably in the ear of the hearer, or in the delivery of the actor. (Whenever we can locate a sexual innuendo in Shakespeare, it is almost certainly there.) Juliet, from her window, does not shy away from the question: 'What satisfaction canst thou have tonight?' (126). Her reply does not so much reject the implied gratification as defer it to a more suitable time. It is Romeo who retreats to propriety: 'Th' exchange of thy love's faithful vow for mine' (127).

Symmetry

The effect of this conversation, then, is the establishment of a parity between the lovers that may defy the expectations of modern audiences, as well as a strong sense of the reciprocity between them. In place of the Petrarchan monologue, most commonly understood to be spoken in solitude by a male lover, the orchard scene presents a dialogue between the couple, where Juliet is allocated more lines than Romeo. Perhaps this impression of symmetry is fostered by the prohibition of women on the public stages. Dressed as a woman but played by a boy, Juliet would look and sound to an early modern audience more like Romeo's equal.

Sixteenth-century education emphasized the difference between the sexes. In elite families, with honourable exceptions, little girls stayed with their mothers and learned the arts of sewing and running a household, alongside whatever they might acquire of reading, writing and foreign languages. Little boys, by contrast, were taken from their mothers' care at the age of six or seven to be taught the masculine skills of horse-riding and fencing, hunting and hawking, as well as Latin – and more Latin. But despite this cultivation of opposite sexes, early modern England notoriously offered women more freedom than many other parts of Europe at the time. And for whatever reason (historical, theatrical, or dramatic), in Shakespeare's plays opposition between the sexes gives way to what we might more appropriately call difference. While sexual difference determines the course of the heterosexual love stories, women characters commonly play a substantial part in the action. This is most noticeable in the comedies where, often disguised as boys, the women may well orchestrate the love scenes, or engineer the final resolution. Moreover, it is Rosalind, not Orlando, who makes the jokes in *As You Like It*; Viola is as witty as the Clown in *Twelfth Night*. Even in the history plays, where war is the province of men, the women complain, intercede and manipulate to considerable effect.

The impression of parity between the lovers in *Romeo and Juliet* is deepened, however, by the effect on Romeo of falling in love. From the Middle Ages on, *courtship* was held to inculcate *courtesy*, the terms sharing a root that originally indicated the good manners appropriate to the *court*, supposedly an island of civilized values in an otherwise barbarous world. Love tamed the wildness of young men. (Young women were already domesticated by their upbringing.) The thirteenth-century French *Romance of the Rose* records this civilizing process in an allegory, translated by Geoffrey Chaucer in the fourteenth century, and by this means available to Shakespeare, in the unlikely event that he needed reminding of such a widespread assumption. In the *Romance* the god of love shoots his arrow at a young man in a delightful garden, and then gives commands to his victim, now love's captive. The youth must forswear bad behaviour of all kinds, be polite to everyone, especially to women, dress as well as he can afford, and be sure to wash his hands, brush his teeth, clean his fingernails, and comb his hair. (Evidently, a sudden teenage interest in the bathroom mirror is only the modern version of ancient custom.) He should also write poems to his lady.

Five years after *Romeo and Juliet* was probably performed, the English essayist William Cornwallis told a similar story:

> It is a pretty soft thing this same love, an excellent company keeper; full of gentleness and affability; makes men fine and go cleanly; teacheth them qualities, handsome protestations; and if the ground be not too barren, it bringeth forth rhymes and songs full of passion.

Romeo, who is capable of the purest poetry, has evidently internalized the appropriate habits. Rosaline, however indifferent to his attentions, at least gave him the chance to rehearse the virtues of courtship – and practice, as we know, makes perfect.

Love brings about a convergence between the sexes. If it reinforces Juliet's courage (makes her brave enough, for example, to take the Friar's potion and face waking up among the dead in the tomb), it not only socializes but also feminizes Romeo, he complains. Newly married to his cousin, Romeo does his best to fend off the insults and challenges of Tybalt, only to find that Mercutio, who knows nothing of his friend's marriage, fights – and dies – on his behalf: 'O sweet Juliet, / Thy beauty hath made me effeminate / And in my temper softened valour's steel' (3.1.115–17). (Even here, Romeo – or his creator – cannot resist a pun. 'Temper' means disposition, temperament; 'tempering' is the process that hardens steel. The Prince has already invoked the same double meaning in his instruction to the rioters, 'Throw your mistempered weapons to the ground' [1.1.85].)

Later, when the news of his banishment brings him close to despair, the Friar will try to induce Romeo to take it like a man (3.3.108–12), adding, 'I thought thy disposition better tempered' (l. 114). The Nurse, too, urges him to 'stand' (89), invoking, whether she knows it or not, all the possible resonances of the word, but not before her observations have drawn attention to the symmetry between the lovers:

> O, he is even in my mistress' case,
> Just in her case. O woeful sympathy,
> Piteous predicament! Even so lies she,
> Blubbering and weeping, weeping and blubbering. (84–7)

The 'woeful sympathy', we are invited to recognize, is a shared experience of unhappiness, common to both and equal in each.

If the company of women had a civilizing effect, it incurred a corresponding danger that it would effeminate men: making love to women saps the masculinity of Antony, as well as Achilles in *Troilus and Cressida*. How unlike our own James Bond and his many stereotypical descendants! In his book about Oscar Wilde, Alan Sinfield gives further examples of the effeminating effects of love in the early modern period, pointing out that they are not generally connected with homoeroticism. Instead, it is the influence of women that does the damage, if damage it is. Comradeship with men brought out masculine values and, Sinfield adds, 'had Romeo been swayed more strongly by his love for Mercutio, that would have been manly'.

Manly it might have been, but where is the play inviting us to place our sympathies? Both Antony and Achilles are first and foremost warriors. Romeo, on the other hand, is not a soldier but a citizen in a feuding society, and love impels him towards peace. This might shame a soldier but in divided Verona it surely constitutes no disgrace. On the contrary. The play offers a foil for Romeo in 'The fiery Tybalt' (1.1.107), whose aggressive masculinity is not in question. He longs to pick a quarrel even at the feast, and roundly declares that he hates the word peace (1.1.68). Would we admire Romeo more, or aspire to be like him, if he were more like Tybalt? In the end, it is (effeminating) love that resolves the feud, but not before (manly) violence has done a good deal more harm. In a violent society bloodshed alters the course of love itself.

Scepticism

Is Romeo's conduct best seen as civilized, or ineffectual, or both? Either way, not everyone in the play shares the idealizing view of love represented by the protagonists. Not everyone outside the play shared it, either. Cornwallis, who praised love's socializing effects, went on to confine the condition to the young, conceding only that it was a better way of passing the time than games of dice. Francis Bacon had even less time for love. In his view, it was fine on the stage, but in real life it did a great deal of mischief, making people behave irrationally.

It also, Bacon complained, made lovers speak 'in a perpetual hyperbole'. Mercutio thinks so too: lovers exaggerate the perfections of the beloved. Not only was Petrarch's lady compared to Romeo's a kitchen wench; Mercutio also mockingly lines up the heroines of the most famous and tragic love stories as equally inadequate by comparison: 'Dido a dowdy, Cleopatra a gypsy, Helen and Hero hildings and harlots, Thisbe a grey eye or so, but not to the purpose' (2.4.41–3). All these women would have been as familiar to many in Shakespeare's audience as Cleopatra – and now Juliet – are to us. They were the legendary material of grammar-school education and contemporary culture: Dido, abandoned by Virgil's epic hero, Aeneas; Helen, abducted by Paris and the cause of the Trojan War; Hero, Leander's lover, whose sad story is told by Christopher Marlowe in a racy poem of the early 1590s; Thisbe, Ovid's protagonist, most memorable now for her absurd impersonation in *A Midsummer Night's Dream*, probably roughly contemporary with *Romeo and Juliet* itself.

Like the sceptical essayists, Mercutio derides love for its folly, its temperamental excesses and its poetry:

Romeo, humours, madman, passion, lover,
Appear thou in the likeness of a sigh,
Speak but one rhyme and I am satisfied.
Cry but 'Ay me', pronounce but 'love' and 'dove',
Speak to my gossip Venus one fair word,
One nickname for her purblind son and heir,
Young Abraham Cupid. (2.1.7–13)

What gives these observations a certain edge is that they come close enough to the actual exchanges between the lovers to act as a comic commentary on the relationship at the heart of the tragedy. Juliet *does* sigh 'Ay me' (2.2.25). No one actually rhymes 'love' and 'dove' (although Hermia does in the contemporary *Midsummer Night's Dream*, 1.1.171–2), but if Juliet does not exactly treat Venus as an intimate, or claim acquaintance with Cupid's first name, she does invoke the goddess as the personification of love in her chariot pulled by doves, as well as her wayward son, in two lines that bring the terms together in an internal rhyme. Desire, Juliet claims in her impatience for news, moves faster than everyday life: 'Therefore do nimble-pinioned doves draw love, / And therefore hath the wind-swift Cupid wings' (2.5.7–8).

Mercutio's aspersions on love intervene between two prolonged lyrical encounters, the first at the feast and the second in the orchard, so that it is hard to escape the element of parody. Where, then, does the play stand on the issue of idealizing passion? Is it, after all, ridiculous, as Mercutio indicates? *Shakespeare in Love* shows Queen Elizabeth enjoying the comedy at a performance of *Two Gentlemen of Verona*, but dozing through the love poetry while Viola is all rapt attention. Perhaps it is a question of point of view: 'He [Mercutio] jests at scars that never felt a wound', Romeo observes without malice (2.2.1). Shakespeare invites his audience to share from the perspective of the lovers themselves the intensity of desire, defined in poetry, but also to stand intermittently outside it and allow its absurdities.

Either way, Mercutio has no hesitation in reducing love to sex:

I conjure thee by Rosaline's bright eyes,
By her high forehead and her scarlet lip,
By her fine foot, straight leg, and quivering thigh
And the demesnes that there adjacent lie. (2.1.17–20)

This is plain talk, without concessions to sighs or classical deities, defining the woman by her body parts, although Mercutio is behind the times: Rosaline has been supplanted. What is more, Mercutio's own rhetoric (since talking dirty is a style like any other) gets worse, or better, according to taste:

Now will he sit under a medlar tree,
And wish his mistress were that kind of fruit
As maids call medlars when they laugh alone.
O Romeo, that she were, O that she were
And open-arse [and] thou a poperin pear! (34–8)

The gist of this is clear enough, especially when the speech is delivered with relish by an actor, but the details bear explanation. The fruit of the *medlar* tree is like a small apple that hollows out at the core as it ripens (a Google image would show what it looks like); it was colloquially known in the period as an *open-arse*. The giggling girls are invoking *meddling*, which means, among other things, sexual activity. And as for a *poperin pear*, this was a long pear with a quintessentially funny name, although, innocently enough in the first instance, it came from Poperinge in Belgium.

In case this low comedy seems remote from the ideal love of the protagonists, it is worth noting that within fifteen lines of Mercutio's 'O, Romeo, that she were, O that she were', we shall hear Romeo himself say, as he gazes at the open window, 'It is my lady, O, it is my love! / O, that she knew she were!' (2.2.10–11), and shortly afterwards, 'O, that I were a glove upon that hand' (24). The proximity of passion and parody risks toppling the poetry on which the love story depends. Only an exceptionally daring author would undertake it – or get away with it, thanks to the sheer inventiveness of the lyricism, its capacity to absorb cliché without toppling into banality.

Shakespeare compounds the risk by investing Juliet's only confidant with a parallel scepticism. Quite apart from her propensity for unconscious sexual innuendo, the Nurse sees marriage for what it mostly is in Verona, a practical matter concerned in the first instance with money. It is from the Nurse that Romeo first learns Juliet's identity, and she adds, 'I tell you, he that can lay hold of her / Shall have the chinks' (1.5.115–16). *Chinks* are both holes and coins: as her father's only heir, Juliet will bring her husband great wealth, as well as sexual pleasure. When it comes to Juliet's projected second marriage, the Nurse takes the pragmatic view. On balance, since Romeo is unlikely to return, 'I think it best you married with the County. / O, he's a lovely gentleman! / Romeo's a dishclout to him' (3.5.218–20). There is surely an echo of Mercutio's comparison between Rosaline and Petrarch's 'kitchen wench'; the difference, however, is that the Nurse means Juliet to believe it.

What is the effect of the Nurse's pragmatism here? To anyone who has been paying attention to the tragedy this far, it is unimaginable that Juliet will take her advice. Does the play, then, by this means give its central figure a chance to make her stance explicit? And does the advice also stand in for the audience's reflections? How bad would it be for Juliet to marry Paris? Very bad, I think, but the Nurse's point of view brings the options out into the open, putting one into the mouth of a speaker whose views, however sympathetic, have already proved less than reliable, all too ready to tack with the wind (see 1.3.76–9; 2.5.39–44).

The Nurse's defection also leaves Juliet even more isolated than before (3.5.240–1), throwing into relief the heroic stance required of an ideal love. Where Romeo's isolation is made actual in his exile from Verona, Juliet's involves a progressive desertion by the members of her household. Separated from each other, the lovers are also cut off from their social context.

Love and the signifier

Before this, however, as they leave the stage to be married, Romeo and Juliet declare their love for each other – or they do their best to do so. But words fall short of the truth, they acknowledge. Romeo begins: if, he appeals to Juliet, you share my joy and have more skill to put it into words, let the 'rich music' that would do it justice 'Unfold the imagined happiness that both / Receive in either by this dear encounter' (2.6.27–9). There is confidence here in the reciprocity of their feelings ('both / Receive in either') with, perhaps, an irony for knowing playgoers in the concession that the happiness to be declared is 'imagined': in practice, any gladness will prove largely imaginary. But Romeo's point is that neither can know for sure the extent of the other's joy without the aid of words as signifiers of a *signified* (meaning). Juliet takes up the thought, but not to solve the problem:

> Conceit more rich in matter than in words
> Brags of his substance, not of ornament.
> They are but beggars that can count their worth,
> But my true love is grown to such excess,
> I cannot sum up sum of half my wealth. (30–4)

'Conceit' (in this instance, what is *conceivable*, the imagined happiness) is proud of its substance, not the poetry that names it; what can be measured or counted out in words is by definition limited, but Juliet's love is immeasurable.

There are two antithetical ways to read this, both, I suggest, justified. On the one hand, the statement that love is beyond words is beyond words romantic, defying the ostensible proposition with *I love you more than words can say*. On the other hand, whatever form it takes, this proposition defines a truth: words can't do it, not even Shakespeare's. Perhaps this is the case for words in general: can we ever say exactly what we mean, once what we mean gets any more complicated than directions to the town centre? But it is especially true in the instance of love, which is not purely conceptual, not just an idea, since it also involves the body, sensation, physiology. Love is the place where mind and body converge, or, to put it for a moment in psychoanalytic terms, where the sexual drive meets culture, as that is inscribed in the meanings we learn to reproduce. Love is expected to gratify at the levels of both sensuality and the highest ideals. If writers go on writing about love, perhaps that is because it poses the supreme challenge to representation.

Love songs might be one place where the signifier begins to do justice to passion, perhaps because they also rely on non-verbal signifiers: sound, rhythm, the physical texture of the voice. Possibly poetry comes closer than prose for much the same reason. *Romeo and Juliet* not only makes one magnificent attempt after another to make passion present to an audience at the level of the signifier; in this exchange between the lovers it also momentarily lays bare the problem all such presentation is obliged to confront. 'I cannot sum up sum of half my wealth': the metaphor (counting riches) and the pun (sum = add, total, part [some]) show language straining its resources of comparison and the multiplication of meanings to achieve what, even so, the play declares finally impossible.

How extraordinary that *Romeo and Juliet*, the most iconic of all love stories, perhaps the definitive representation of passion, should pronounce its theme beyond definition! Nevertheless, the speech in which the newly married Juliet impatiently foresees their wedding night goes as far as language can towards overcoming the obstacles (3.2.1–31). 'Gallop apace, you fiery-footed steeds, / Towards Phoebus' lodging' (1–2), the home of the sun-god. The speeding horses of the opening lines enact the urgency of desire and the rhythm of its impulse. Mythologically speaking, Phoebus Apollo drove his golden chariot across the sky each day and, as it sank from view in the west, darkness returned to the earth. Juliet goes on to appeal to night to draw the curtain of darkness, figured as the bed-hangings, round the couple, so that Romeo may 'leap' to her arms in secret, 'untalked of and unseen'. Lovers do not need light: they 'can see to do their amorous rites / By their own beauties'; their perceptions are tactile, sensual. The lines incorporate and at the same time idealize the sexuality Mercutio has cynically isolated from love: 'Come, civil night ... And learn me how to lose a winning match / Played for a pair of stainless maidenhoods'; night is to cover Juliet's hitherto 'unmanned' blushes, 'till strange love grow bold'. 'Civil' is unexpected here: Juliet flatters the darkness by calling it polite, the preserver of propriety, while the act it is to conceal will initially be 'strange', unfamiliar to the innocent lovers, but also out of the ordinary, special – and increasingly 'bold', confident, daring.

Coincidentally or not, in 1595 Edmund Spenser published his own marriage song, *Epithalamion.* The poem traces the events of the wedding day until it reaches the evening and the impatience of the bridegroom, and now it begins to overlap with Juliet's speech: 'Ah when will this long weary day have end?' 'Haste thee', the husband urges the sun, 'to thy home / Within the Westerne fome. / Thy tyred steeds long since have need of rest' (lines 278, 282–4). At last the bride is ushered into their bedroom. 'Now welcome night, thou night so long expected', the groom exclaims; 'Spread thy broad wing over my love and me, / That no man may us see' (315, 319–20), as they share 'sweet snatches of delight' (362). The male author, we are to understand, is the speaker here. Surprisingly, radically, Shakespeare ascribes his more compressed and more sexually explicit epithalamion to a woman.

Juliet's speech, at the mid-point of the play, ends with the entry of the Nurse, who wrings her hands at Tybalt's death. It occurs at the climactic moment of the lovers' imagined happiness: from now on, that joy will be more and more evidently threatened, and love more closely imbricated with death.

Writing matters

Now it is time to continue building your file of commentary by close attention to another passage. The first exchanges between Romeo and Juliet at the feast take the form of a sonnet (1.5.92–105) – another sonnet to compare with the Prologue, but this time a way for Romeo to solicit a response. The sonnet form usually presents itself as a private utterance, the lyrical enunciation of personal feeling, and critics have made the point that their intense colloquy here separates the lovers from the bustle of the party. If in the case of the Prologue, Shakespeare modified the convention to turn a lyric form into narrative, here he transforms what is usually monologue into exchanges between two voices, culminating in a kiss. How are the parts allotted in such a way that the sonnet structure of three quatrains and a couplet is preserved and yet the voices differ? And what are the implications for the reciprocity and the symmetry the play creates between its protagonists?

What kind of love is it that is formulated in a vocabulary of shrines, pilgrims, saints and prayer? And what are we to make of the inclusion of 'sin', albeit 'gentle', and the 'profane' possibilities of touching? Above all, how far can it be said that the wordplay enacts the playful teasing of an encounter between lovers? Bear in mind that *pilgrims*, who worshipped (statues of) *saints*, were also known as *palmers* because, if they got as far as Jerusalem, they conventionally carried palm branches back.

We generally think of a sonnet as a written text, circulated in the early modern period in manuscript in the first instance. Francis Meres commented in 1598 on Shakespeare's 'sugared sonnets among his private friends'. What happens when a written genre is brought to life in the theatre? Even though there are no original stage directions at this point (any that appear in modern editions are placed there by later editors), how should we imagine the body language of the actors here? How would you expect them to move? What do the lines encourage them to do?

Finally, the following four lines begin another sonnet, but this is interrupted when Juliet is summoned to her mother. Is the Nurse simply doing her job as chaperone, or does the abrupt termination of the lovers' exchanges foreshadow the future of their story?

Give it time: more observations take shape the longer you concentrate on the passage. And for future reference, it is worth noting explicitly that you are looking closely at *vocabulary*, *puns*, and *structure*, with an eye to the way an individual passage relates to the *conventional* textual practices of the period. The project is to make the short extract demonstrate something about the way the play sets out to engage the audience in its concerns. Although you may need help with the conventions (specifically, in this instance, my earlier comments on the sonnet genre), all the rest relies on you and the text, with the aid of notes or a dictionary to alert you to usages that have become unfamiliar in the intervening 400 years.

CHAPTER THREE

The language of death

Lovers of the night

Romeo and Juliet appear on stage together four times in the course of the play. One of these meetings takes place in daylight at the Friar's cell and leads to their marriage; the others are conducted under the cover of darkness. Moreover, even these encounters are interrupted by pressures and demands from the outside, everyday world beyond the lovers' control. Prohibited, obstructed, driven to secrecy, theirs is in every sense a love that belongs to solitude and the night.

Their courtship relinquishes the conventional forms of display. At the feast where the couple first meet, for example, they do not in the event dance: the nurse summons Juliet to her mother instead. Although they kiss, apparently no one sees them do so. The moment might be seen as epitomizing their relationship: an intense exchange between the protagonists takes place apart, effectively independent of the activities that surround them; the play cancels the visible, social activity of dancing together among the other partygoers.

Dancing showed itself to the world. In *The Governour*, his book about education published in 1531, Sir Thomas Elyot took issue with puritanical opponents of this pastime. Formal dancing, a man and a woman moving together in time and in harmony, involved a discipline, he argued; the necessary concord between the couple offered an image of marriage.

Four hundred years later T. S. Eliot liked this passage from his ancestor's book well enough to cite it in his poem 'East Coker': 'The association of man and woman / In daunsinge, signifying matrimonie'. Marriage, too, showed itself publicly, this time as a promise of fidelity in the presence of witnesses, made before God but declared to society. In one sense, then, a hidden marriage, 'untalked of and unseen' (3.2.7), is a contradiction in terms. While dancing is open, communal, and marriage belongs to legality and the light of day, the union of Romeo and Juliet takes place behind the back of their social group, concealed by the night.

Marriage also depends on the absence of impediments. The Elizabethan Book of Common Prayer, which ordered the conduct of religious ceremonies, required the clergyman to publish banns for three separate Sundays before the solemnization of matrimony. He was to urge parishioners to come forward with any information they possessed that would constitute an obstacle to the contract: a prior marriage to a living partner, or close kinship between the pair, for example. In the course of the ceremony itself, the same injunction would be put to the couple: 'if either of you do know any impediment, why ye may not be lawfully joined together in matrimony, that ye confess it'. Shakespeare alludes to the wording in Sonnet 116, 'Let me not to the marriage of true minds / Admit impediment', although here the barred impediment is psychological, not legal.

Although no legal impediments forbid their marriage, obstructions imposed by society consistently impede the relationship between Romeo and Juliet. In the orchard the lovers are separated, Romeo within the walled garden that encloses and secures Juliet's chastity but Juliet above at her 'window'. We assume that early modern productions placed Juliet in the gallery, while Romeo spoke from below on the main stage. In the eighteenth century, when the gallery had disappeared, productions emphasized this physical separation by introducing a balcony as the impediment that visibly divides them (and that will separate them once again when they part in 3.5). His presence in the garden threatens Romeo with death (2.2.64), while the exchanges in the dark, lyrical and passionate though they are, momentarily fill Juliet with foreboding: 'Although I joy in thee / I have no joy of this contract tonight; / It is too rash, too unadvised, too sudden' (116–18). Even Romeo fears that their midnight encounter has been no more substantial than a dream (139–41).

In this instance the dialogue between the lovers is repeatedly interrupted by the calls of the Nurse: twice Juliet returns to continue their conversation until the third parting. If the device is engaging, comic even, as a comment on love's irrepressible urgency, it is also prophetic, a foretaste of things to come. Their conduct, it makes evident, will not be at their own disposal.

Juliet is alone when she imagines their wedding night. At the level of realism this is perfectly plausible: a bride, parted temporarily from her new husband, looks forward to their 'unseen' union in the dark; under the shelter of night, they will make love by the light of their own beauty (3.2.7–9). In the context of the story, however, Juliet's solitude at this important moment is intelligible as ominous: the couple will spend more of their short married life in the open but on their own than with each other, where they must be invisible.

When they re-enter together as dawn breaks, they do so only to separate once more, divided this time by Verona's law, interrupted again by the Nurse, who comes to warn them that Lady Capulet is coming, and parted above all by the advent of morning. The light of day is now explicitly a threat. They will die in the darkness of the tomb, lit only – in a way that echoes the imagined wedding night – by Juliet's beauty (5.3.85–6) and, ironically, alone again: in the same place but separately.

The letters kills

Like the delights of love (2.6.30–4), the pain of separation exceeds the signifier: '"Romeo is banished" – / There is no end, no limit, measure, bound, / In that word's death; no words can that woe sound' (3.2.124–6), where to *sound* is to measure the depth and to make audible. To put it differently, Juliet cannot utter a sentence that does justice to the effect on her of the sentence on Romeo pronounced by the Prince; words fall short of defining the agony that, paradoxically, the word can cause when it becomes law. If love, felt by the organism on the pulses, in the flesh, cannot be adequately represented, suffering, experienced physiologically as weeping, prostration, is also beyond the reach of the signifier.

The letter of the law parts the protagonists but in the first instance it is their names that doom their love. Names, given by parents to their children, bring with them a place in the social world, in this instance dividing lovers from each other. 'Deny thy father and refuse thy name', urges Juliet (2.2.34). 'Or if thou wilt not, be but sworn my love, / And I'll no longer be a Capulet' (35–6). Since their union is afforded no place in the feuding community that impels them to hate each other, Juliet imagines a realm of pure love outside social exchange, beyond the reach of words: "Tis but thy name that is my enemy. / Thou art thyself' (2.2.38–9). Surely Romeo would be the self he is, Juliet reflects, whatever his appellation. 'What's in a name?' (43). It is not, after all, integral, not like a hand, or a foot, or any other part that belongs to a man. Romeo is her enemy only on the grounds that her name is Capulet. What have their names to do with passion, where one organism encounters another, one self 'takes' another (49)? Doesn't love, which exceeds the signifier, also suspend it? 'That which we call a rose / By any other word would smell as sweet; / So Romeo would, were he not Romeo called' (44–5).

Is she right? Could Romeo 'doff' his name (47), take it off like a hat, and still be himself? What is a self? Can it be so easily divorced from a name? How does a self compare with the rose that Juliet selects as her example? Roses signify. The sweet smell of the rose, appropriately invoked here as a comparator for Romeo because it is associated by long poetic tradition with love and youth and beauty, might retain those connotations if it were known by any other word, but not if it were name-less, unable to be identified repeatedly in countless love poems. Continuing conventions of this kind are by definition shared; the distinctive signifying properties of the rose are known in language. True, the scent of the rose is organic, but it is thanks to the signifier that we recognize its specific, inherited meaning.

The play indicates that for speaking beings, too, there is no way of specifying selfhood outside the signifier. To make known his presence in the orchard as he overhears Juliet's reflections, Romeo speaks. Punning, he offers to change his name: 'Call me but love and I'll be new baptized' (50). Juliet presses the point, however: who is he, this man who is inside the walled garden of the Capulets and has heard her secrets in the dark? 'By a name', Romeo replies, 'I know not how to tell thee who I am' (53–4); 'Had I it written, I would tear the word' (57). If, on the one hand, he is reluctant to identify himself by the word that is his name, unnamed, on the other, he cannot distinguish himself from the predators and thieves who might have more sinister business in the orchard. Anonymity is not an option. In the event, Juliet knows his voice and confirms her recognition in the readiest way: 'Art thou not Romeo, and a Montague?' (60). *Romeo* is his proper name, the name that properly belongs to him, even though it was conferred by his parents, the Montagues, without his intervention. This name, tying him to his heritage in society, is also the acknowledgement of his individuality in it.

Love is personal, a relationship between individuals; the names that differentiate them are more, therefore, than incidental. Named, however, Romeo faces danger. Paradoxically, the word that marks out the person Juliet loves also signifies enmity, because it denominates a family, incurring consequences that are not under individual control: the place is death 'considering who thou art' (64). *Romeo* is who he is – and a *Montague*. Words, which apparently only symbolize the selves they name, in practice bring with them a whole social order that those selves cannot by an act of individual will choose not to inhabit. Technically, perhaps Romeo could be called something else ('O be some other name!' [42]) just as the rose could, but that would not by itself exclude him from the Montague lineage he was born to and the hostility to the Capulets traditionally attached to it. The feud inherited with the names, the hatred that is not individual, will prove inescapable until the two families repudiate it. But by then the lovers are dead, 'Poor sacrifices of [their] enmity' (5.3.304).

In the course of the play Juliet unilaterally offers to rename the lark a nightingale and call the rising sun a meteor (3.5) but she cannot by this means postpone for one instant the morning that is marked by the lark's song and the sunrise, the dawn that in turn signifies the moment of Romeo's banishment. There is, it seems, no realm of pure love outside the world of names and words, while meanings are inherited, not at the disposal of the individual or, indeed, the couple. Language that is the condition of this relationship is also the obstacle to its survival: only a change in the social order would have modified the meaning of their names and released Romeo and Juliet to choose one another.

When that change finally comes, reconciliation is registered both in words – 'O brother Montague', exclaims Old Capulet (5.3.296) – and in actions – they take hands and reciprocally promise the golden effigies. Oddly enough, this eventual peace is secured in the name of the city:

> For I will raise her statue in pure gold,
> That whiles Verona by that name is known,
> There shall no figure at such rate be set
> As that of true and faithful Juliet. (5.3.299–302)

At first glance, this reference to their town seems no more than a rhetorical flourish, a way of dignifying the concluding lines. But possibly the allusion is more than incidental. Perhaps we are invited to notice that the warring names of Montague and Capulet are now subsumed under the single name of the community they will unify by the new way they speak and conduct themselves.

Genre

If the love of Romeo and Juliet is constantly obstructed, obstacles need not lead to tragedy: comedy, too, depends on impediments. Structurally, the first half of *Romeo and Juliet* might lead the audience to expect a happy ending. The Latin comedies that would have been familiar from Shakespeare's grammar-school education conventionally depended on lovers forbidden to marry, often by a heavy father. A sympathetic servant would side with the young people and help them find ways round their difficulty, and there would in the process be a good deal of satirical comment concerning a society driven by greed and aggression.

On this classical basis Renaissance Italy developed the *commedia dell'arte* (the comedy of skill, because its success depended to a high degree on the craft of the performers). The genre, which spread rapidly throughout Europe from the middle of the sixteenth century, presented standard figures in a variety of situations, among them young lovers, ingenious servants, and an old father, *Pantalone*, the pantaloon, who puts in a brief appearance as one of the seven ages in *As You Like It* (2.7.158). In line with his name, Pantaloon was commonly a figure of fun.

At roughly the same time as Shakespeare was writing *Romeo and Juliet*, he must have been working on *A Midsummer Night's Dream*, which makes comedy out of a father who arbitrarily insists that his daughter prefer his choice of suitor to her own. Modern rom com, which owes a great deal to Shakespeare and ultimately to classical comedy, similarly tends to present an obstacle to love that is eventually overcome to provide a happy ending. Old Capulet, the party-giver, hospitable, gossipy, reminded by his wife that a crutch would suit him better than a sword, initially appears more absurd than threatening. The malapropisms of the garrulous, well-meaning but ultimately unromantic Nurse/servant seem cut out for situation comedy, while the young men who have nothing more pressing to do than exchange one-liners anticipate Woody Allen.

Romeo and Juliet could just as well end with the triumph of the lovers over adversity, or so some critics have suggested. The tragic ending is accidental: if the Friar's letter had reached Romeo before the news that Juliet was dead, the couple might have escaped from the tomb together, left behind their fractured community and lived happily ever after in Mantua. The British theatre company Headlong produced the play in 2012 to emphasize the element of chance in the plot. Successive episodes were repeated with a difference, in the manner of such films as *Sliding Doors* and *Groundhog Day*, to bring out how much in the play depends on hazard. Suppose, for example, the servant detailed to invite the guests to the Capulet feast had been able to read: Romeo would never have met Juliet. What if Paris, deflected from his courtship of Juliet by Tybalt's death, had packed his bags and left? A stage direction seems to glimpse that possibility: '*Paris offers to go in and Capulet calls him again*' (3.4.11SD). In the Headlong version Friar John reached Romeo with the letter summoning him to rescue Juliet – and then didn't.

Mischance, coincidence, unexpected solutions are more often characteristic of comedy, where fairies confuse one mortal with another, lovers happen to flee at the same moment to the same forest, and long-lost brothers turn up in the nick of time. But genre is not purely a question of plot. *A Midsummer Night's Dream* dramatizes as high comedy the sad tale of Pyramus and Thisbe. Told by Ovid in the *Metamorphoses*, Shakespeare's favourite Latin text, their story closely parallels the plot of *Romeo and Juliet*. Similarly forbidden to marry, Pyramus and Thisbe too are reduced to conducting their relationship in secret. Mistakenly believing Thisbe dead, Pyramus kills himself and she, finding his body, takes the same course. If Shakespeare's treatment of these tragic events evokes tears, however, they are sure to be tears of laughter. I have seen many productions of *A Midsummer Night's Dream*, some of them more competent than others, but even the most inadequate amateur performance can hardly fail to make this play-within-the-play funny.

What, then, makes the difference between the genres? First, the treatment of events. For one thing, comedy keeps its audience at arm's length. However much we are encouraged to sympathize with the protagonists, we are also invited to observe their emotions from a place outside them. This depends not so much on the comments of others as on the way the characters speak. The dialogue between Pyramus and Thisbe is a jumble of misunderstood conventions and outmoded banalities. Unable to command the language of love, they hold the audience at an ironic distance from their feelings. Even the lyrical exchanges between the romantic lovers in *A Midsummer Night's Dream* are much more conventional, far less risky, than the love poetry of *Romeo and Juliet*. Involved, by contrast, in the grand emotions of these tragic protagonists, whose soaring poetry makes them seem larger than life, we are encouraged to see events from their point of view.

We might choose to detect a generic points-switch when death enters the tragedy directly. Mercutio dies by accident ('Why the devil came you between us? I was hurt under your arm' [3.1.104–5]) and with a bleak joke ('Ask for me tomorrow and you shall find me a grave man' [99–100]). Mercurial, as his name suggests, flamboyant, extravagant, Mercutio owes something to the Harlequin of the *commedia dell'arte*, the colourful, irrepressible, agile figure who entertains the audience by talking brilliantly about nothing very much; he also stands in a line of descent from the earthy clown of Elizabethan comedy, who fools with language for its own sake. On Mercutio's death the possibility of a happy outcome seems to diminish along with the light-heartedness. From then on there is less room for optimism: Romeo becomes a killer;

the lovers are separated, Romeo isolated in Mantua and Juliet increasingly alone in Verona; Old Capulet morphs into a tyrant and the Nurse aligns herself with her employers. Only the Friar remains constant to the lovers and he cannot, in the event, save the day. The second half of the play dramatizes Juliet's solitary fear of the effects of the Friar's potion ('My dismal scene I needs must act alone' [4.3.19]) and the lamentations for her supposed death (4.5), with the result that the rhetorical movement of the tragedy towards the tomb now seems all but irresistible.

Prolepsis

In addition, however, the play includes repeated allusions to the ending. Proleptic images – prefiguring events that have not yet taken place – remind the audience of what is to follow. Tragedy generally inculcates a sense of doom, inevitability: from the moment Hamlet sees the Ghost or Macbeth the witches, the audience is entitled to expect the worst. Perhaps precisely because the outcome of *Romeo and Juliet* does not initially seem inevitable, because it is accidental, this play keeps its conclusion in perpetual view from the Prologue on. Ominously, Romeo senses in advance, for instance, that the Capulet feast will unaccountably issue in 'Some consequence, yet hanging in the stars' (1.4.107) and lead in a way he cannot fathom to 'untimely death' (111). Only one proleptic statement emphasizes the positive conclusion. Undertaking to marry the lovers, Friar Laurence explains why he is ready to take so unconventional a step: 'this alliance may so happy prove, / To turn your households' rancour to pure love' (2.3.87–8). Such an effect is not all that improbable: marriages commonly confirmed the treaties between warring nations, as *Henry V* demonstrates. Indeed, this marriage will fulfil the Friar's hope – eventually. But playgoers are entitled to recognize, from the Prologue, perhaps because they already know the story, but also from the manner of the exchanges between the lovers, that there will be a high price to pay for the promised reconciliation.

Other proleptic utterances are less reassuring. Already in Act 1, directly after the first meeting between the lovers, an irony is available to attentive members of the audience when Juliet brings together marriage and death: 'Go ask his name. If he be married, / My grave is like to be my wedding bed' (1.5.133–4). At this moment it is as if death enters into her declaration of love, already has its place there as a possible outcome. Juliet's tomb and her marriage bed will be conflated in ways she cannot yet foresee, although a knowing audience can.

Allusions to the tomb will recur as the obstacles accumulate. 'I would the fool were married to her grave', exclaims Lady Capulet, impatient that Juliet resists the marriage her father has planned for her (3.5.140). To the speaker this is simply a way of formulating her anger; to an astute audience it anticipates what is to come. Later in the scene, Juliet's threat again foreshadows the same fate: 'Delay this marriage for a month, a week, / Or if you do not, make the bridal bed / In that dim monument where Tybalt lies' (200–2). The vault already holds itself out as Juliet's best effort to remain faithful to love.

As he urges the Friar to marry them, Romeo delivers a challenge to the future: 'Do thou but close our hands with holy words, / Then love-devouring death do what he dare' (2.6.6–7). Once again death represents a component part of the commitment to love. Is this a poetic way of promising to love Juliet till death them do part? Or is it something more? An image of devouring *time* was familiar from Ovid's *Metamorphoses*, source-book for the best-known early modern love stories and tales of transformation. The last book of the *Metamorphoses* concerns the greatest transformer of them all, gluttonous time that destroys beauty and leads to extinction. Even the world itself is in perpetual flux. 'Tempus edax rerum', Ovid complains (literally, time, greedy eater of things). 'Time, you great devourer, and you, envious age, together you destroy everything, and, slowly gnawing with your teeth, little by little you consume all things in lingering death' (15.234–6). Shakespeare alludes to this by now proverbial passage in Sonnet 19: 'Devouring time, blunt thou the lion's paws'. But Romeo's 'love-devouring death' speeds up what in Ovid is a gradual, protracted process: time disappears from his phrase to bring passion and destruction together, compressing their connection into a single and contradictory instant.

The image of death as a mouth consuming living things would make sense to an audience already familiar with the traditional representation of the jaws of hell. Paint and stained glass in parish churches depicted – or had depicted until recently, when the Reformation decreed that such imagery be painted over – a vision of the Last Judgement, when the dead would rise from their graves and face their Maker. The damned would be hustled into an inferno entered by means of huge open maw with powerful teeth. 'Ugly hell, gape not!' Marlowe's Dr Faustus had exclaimed, as he faced death on the stage only two or three years before *Romeo and Juliet*. Philip Henslowe, owner of the Rose theatre, kept records of his company's costumes and properties. In 1598, two or three years after Shakespeare's play was performed at the Theatre, the Rose possessed '1 hell mouth', listed, as luck would have it, alongside '1 tomb'.

The last words of the living lovers to each other foreshadow their next and final encounter. As Juliet looks down from her window at Romeo, who has descended the rope ladder that gave him access to her bedroom, she wonders anxiously whether they will ever meet again. He hastens to reassure her but she is not convinced:

> O God, I have an ill-divining soul!
> Methinks I see thee, now thou art so low,
> As one dead in the bottom of a tomb. (3.5.54–6)

The image of the dead Romeo will soon recur, this time subject to multiple levels of irony. Eager to convince her mother that her tears are for Tybalt's death and that she hates

Romeo as his murderer, Juliet insists, 'Indeed, I never shall be satisfied / With Romeo till I behold him. Dead – / Is my poor heart so for a kinsman vexed' (3.5.93–5). These lines take some unpicking. The project is to mislead but not to lie: if the signifier is not at our disposal, we can at least assert ourselves to exploit its potential duplicity. Juliet's equivocations depend on the supposed punctuation, which is hard to reproduce on the page. On the stage, however, where punctuation marks are not visible, the alternative options rely on the actor's delivery. As far as Lady Capulet is concerned, the meaning offered is: *I shall never be satisfied with Romeo till I behold him … dead; my heart is dead, so afflicted is it with grief for my cousin*. But the truth concealed in this is very different: *I shall never have had enough of Romeo until I see him (again); my heart is dead with grief for my harried husband*. Are playgoers expected to grasp the full sense of both meanings? I'm not certain. But what they would surely not miss is the proleptic allusion to the tragic ending: till I behold him … dead.

Death personified

One subset of these proleptic images is more shocking than the others. Paris comes to accompany his bride. She is ready to go to the church, laments her father, but not to be married. Instead,

> O son, the night before thy wedding day
> Hath death lain with thy wife. There she lies,
> Flower as she was, deflowered by him.
> Death is my son-in-law, death is my heir.
> My daughter he hath wedded. (4.5.35–9)

This macabre perception of death personified as a bridegroom taking possession of Juliet's virgin body is not an isolated instance. Convinced that Romeo is already banished before the consummation of their marriage, Juliet protests 'I'll to my wedding bed / And death, not Romeo, take my maidenhead' (3.2.136–7).

These images would have had a special resonance for early modern playgoers. Their society was more familiar with death than our own. Life expectancy was low; before the discovery of antibiotics, infections could be devastating; childbirth was perpetually hazardous. Plague periodically swept through London: 1593–4 saw a major outbreak shortly before Shakespeare must have started work on the play. Young and old died at home, often in great pain. In response, early modern culture depicted the exterminator with a mixture of fear and mockery: well into the seventeenth century the figure of Death was a familiar iconographic image. Church decoration, sophisticated woodcuts and cheap prints alike portrayed him as an emaciated, skeletal or desiccated carcass, a dead body but paradoxically alive and energetic, skipping, grinning, gloating over his victims. Does the play allow us to glimpse his avatar in the death-dealing Apothecary? 'Meagre were his looks, / Sharp misery had worn him to the bones', and again, 'Famine is in thy cheeks, / Need and oppression starveth in thine eyes' (5.1.40–1, 69–70).

All over Europe Dances of Death showed a variety of such gaunt figures as they seized living partners. No one was immune. The Dance might be led by an emperor, a pope or a king in the grip of a cadaver; it ended with a beggar or a fool clutched in another bony hand. In between, all ages and classes of society, as well as both sexes, were dragged from their everyday activities to cavort with a capering mummy.

When Sir Thomas Elyot defended dancing, he knew that he wrote against powerful clerical condemnation of that pastime's erotic possibilities. The Dance of Death exploited the sexual implications of its own iconography: Death embraced his living partners as he whirled them into the procession against their will; this grotesque reveller practised a seduction that could not be resisted. When Capulet depicts death deflowering his daughter, when Juliet imagines death taking her maidenhead, they draw on a well-established association between death and love.

Half a century later, in the poem addressed 'To his Coy Mistress', Andrew Marvell was to threaten his own cruel fair with a deadly defloration: 'Then worms shall try / That long-preserved virginity'. In the Capulet tomb a desperate Romeo perceives worms as Juliet's chambermaids (5.3.109) but not before he too has imagined death as her lover:

> Ah, dear Juliet
> Why art thou yet so fair? Shall I believe
> That unsubstantial death is amorous,
> And that the lean abhorred monster keeps
> Thee here in dark to be his paramour? (101–5)

The irony here – there is a quite different explanation for Juliet's continuing vitality, if only Romeo could perceive it – does not detract from the grim image of death as a sexual predator. (Cleopatra is evidently familiar with the connection too: 'The stroke of death is as a lover's pinch / Which hurts and is desired' [*Antony and Cleopatra*, 5.2.293–4]). When Death featured as a lone figure in the imagery of the period, he might carry a shaft, for all the world like a cadaverous Cupid whose arrow is phallic as well as fatal. Ben Jonson's last play would include a song invoking a polite version of the analogy:

> Though I am young, and cannot tell,
> Either what Death or Love is well,
> Yet I have heard they both bear darts
> And both do aim at human hearts.

Love and death

Was early modern iconography on to something? Is there a link between love and death? Psychoanalysis would say so.

Sigmund Freud struggled with the idea that two fundamental drives impelled human behaviour: on the one hand, the sexual impulse to pleasure and the creation of new life; on the other, the death drive, projected outwards as hate. The more Freud looked into this idea, the more difficult he found it to keep the two drives apart. It was his successor Jacques Lacan who resolved the problem by combining the two imperatives in a single drive that might issue in either passionate love or deadly hate, the two sometimes inextricably entwined. Our strongest emotions may each include a trace of the other in whichever seems uppermost.

Shakespeare's play gives a hint of a similar understanding in Juliet's reaction to Tybalt's death. Her first response is to blame Romeo: 'O serpent heart hid with a flowering face ... Beautiful tyrant, fiend angelical, / Dove-feather'd raven, wolvish-ravening lamb' (3.2.73–6). Her rage and disappointment are not only in proportion to the intensity of her love, they also keep that love in view, even in the ferocity of her condemnation: Romeo is as irresistible as he is deadly. When she brings antithetical feelings into conjunction here, Juliet's utterances evoke the familiar Petrarchan paradoxes, and each oxymoron inscribes a duality of feeling that resembles Romeo's frustrated desire for Rosaline: 'O brawling love, O loving hate ... This love feel I that feel no love in this' (1.1.174–80). Is it possible that the play owes something of its iconic stature to the fact that its plot brings into the open the familiar proximity of contradictory emotions: 'My only love sprung from my only hate' (1.5.137)? Lovers' quarrels have a special intensity: the rage is in proportion to the love because the stakes are so high. Why are some divorces so very acrimonious? Perhaps because only love disappointed, betrayed, or lost issues in such unappeasable fury.

Juliet's anger concerning Tybalt soon gives way to desolation at Romeo's banishment, a source of woe equivalent to ten thousand dead Tybalts (3.2.114). Now her sorrow is infinite: 'There is no end, no limit, measure, bound / In that word's death' (125–6). Love thwarted is deadly to her; death is concealed in love itself, repressed in the good times but ready to break out as hatred or self-destruction when things go wrong. In the end, deprived, as he believes, of Juliet, Romeo will choose to swallow poison. Cheated of a future for her love, Juliet will take on herself the action of Death's dart when she stabs herself with Romeo's dagger.

Could it be otherwise? Suppose for a moment that Romeo and Juliet do not die. Can we imagine them furnishing a house and selecting schools for their children? Is it possible to think of Romeo performing the Elizabethan equivalent of pushing the trolley while Juliet chooses breakfast cereals at the supermarket? In a provocative essay, widely anthologized, 'Romeo and Juliet: Love-Hatred in the Couple', the psychoanalyst Julia Kristeva assesses the proximity of love and death in the play. There is much in what she says to disagree with, but one passage has given me pause for considerable thought. If we conceive of the lovers' survival, Kristeva argues, there are two possibilities for them:

> Either time's alchemy transforms the criminal, secret passion of the outlaw lovers into the banal, humdrum, lackluster lassitude of a tired and cynical collusion: that is the normal marriage. Or else the married couple continues to be a passionate couple, but covering the entire gamut of sadomasochism that the two partners already heralded in the yet relatively quiet version of the Shakespearean text.

Her point here is that, thanks to the proximity of love and hate, passion is by definition at odds with community. Long-term partnership is legitimate, public, its domesticity a concession to civil society. It is moderate, as the Friar advises (2.6.14); such a relationship inhabits the everyday world. *Romeo and Juliet* belongs to another tradition, the heritage of heroic love stories where prohibition of one kind or another intensifies love to the point of desperation. For Virgil's Dido and Aeneas, Chaucer's Troilus and Criseyde, Shakespeare's own Antony and Cleopatra, settling down together is not an option. These figures preserve the legendary grandeur of their love, its absolute commitment, along with its capacity for (self-)destruction, by staying aloof from marriage and domesticity. Since, Kristeva argues, Romeo and Juliet do marry, Shakespeare maintains the propriety of the institution by curtailing it: 'having them die, he saved the pure couple. He safeguarded the innocence of marriage under the shroud of death.'

Kristeva opens her essay with a reference to Denis de Rougemont's *Love in the Western World*, first published in French in 1939. This influential work argues that love stories are moving to the degree that they bring romance into relation with death. Happy love, Rougemont repeatedly insists, has no history, no story. What produces the most profound intensity, the greatest lyricism and the most compelling narrative, is a fatal passion. 'And passion means suffering.' His etymology is accurate: 'the Passion' is a synonym for the Christian crucifixion. Romantic comedy, while it pleases, is perhaps more easily forgotten than the tragic narratives that, like *Romeo and Juliet* itself, are repeatedly reread, rewritten, and reinterpreted. Even so, it is worth noting that romantic comedy classically stops at or before the wedding; this genre preserves the propriety of married life by deferring it.

And, meanwhile, tragic love protects itself from dwindling into domesticity, preserving its own sublimity by accumulating impediments. The poet W. H. Auden, who reviewed Rougemont's book enthusiastically, borrows its framework to read Shakespeare's play:

> Now the obstacle that the lovers ideally require must be insurmountable. That is to say, their union must be possible only through their deaths. This is the secret, the religious mystery, of Romantic Love, the mystery that is represented by the suicides of Romeo and Juliet.

The current English title of Rougemont's book does justice to the original French (*L'Amour et l'Occident*: Love and the West) but the first British imprint of the translation called it *Passion and Society*. That title captures not only a crucial implication of its argument but also the theme of Shakespeare's tragedy, where the lovers are driven deeper into the darkness of a desire that is all the more intense because it is outlawed by their community. In the tomb Romeo seals with a last kiss 'A dateless bargain to engrossing death' (5.3.115). There will be no agreed term, no settlement date, with this opponent, as death engrosses (absorbs, encompasses) the couple forever. *Engross* carries a range of meanings in the period, all condensed here into a single metaphor. To engross is to draw up a legal document or a contract, to take possession of land or property, and to fatten, make *gross*. The lovers, menaced from the first by a fatality perceived as devouring, can find rest for ever (110) only as their last embrace (113) is encompassed in turn by gluttonous death.

Sex and violence

When Romeo delivers his challenge to love-devouring death, Friar Laurence registers a link between passion and gunpowder: such fervent intensities have catastrophic outcomes, he warns, 'like fire and powder / Which, as they kiss, consume' (2.6.10–11). The play does not let its audience forget the association between love and the threat of violence. It is while Romeo first sees Juliet's beauty and resolves to take her by the hand that Tybalt sends for his rapier with a view to killing him (1.5.54–8). When Juliet declares her longing for the wedding night, although she does not know it, Mercutio and Tybalt are newly dead. At the same time, in that speech the association between love and death is also more intimate; an image of disaster inhabits sex itself in her challenge to the sun-god's galloping horses to increase their pace towards the darkness she yearns for: 'Such a wagoner / As Phaeton would whip you to the west / And bring in cloudy night immediately' (3.2.2–4).

According to the myth related by Ovid, young Phaeton, son of Phoebus Apollo, demanded to be allowed to drive his father's chariot of the sun across the sky, but he was not capable of commanding Apollo's powerful steeds, lacking, as Richard II was to put it, 'the manage of unruly jades' (3.3.179). The sun-god's magnificent horses ran out of control, the earth was singed, the chariot wrecked and Phaeton hurled headlong to the earth in flames. The consummation of this marriage is as reckless, as dangerous, as the short journey of Phaeton's careering horses. If Juliet's allusion to the story points to the surrender of restraint that will characterize the sexual encounter between the newly-weds, if it indicates the riskiness of this first-ever night of love, conducted in secret, it also echoes the Friar's association of passion with mortality: 'These violent delights have violent ends / And in their triumph die' (2.6.9–10).

The Prologue has already brought procreation and death together in its image of the star-crossed lovers sprung from 'fatal loins' (5) and the opening scene goes on to associate sex with fatality of another kind. The brawl links rape and death in Sampson's boast: 'I will show myself a tyrant: when I have fought with the men, I will be civil with the maids, I will cut off their heads ... or their maidenheads, take it in what sense thou wilt' (1.1.20–5). Tyranny issues in defloration. There are still parts of the world where rape constitutes an element of warfare. Apparently, it confirms the masculinity of the victors (there's evidently no danger of effeminacy in so brief a contact with women). At the same time, it demoralizes the opposing forces by demonstrating that the men are unable to protect their wives and daughters from humiliation, while arresting in the process the lineage of the conquered people. The two servants find this joke about taking maidenheads well worth sustaining:

> *Gregory.* They must take it in sense that feel it.
> *Sampson.* Me they shall feel while I am able to stand, and 'tis known I am a pretty piece of flesh. (26–8)

As the Montagues appear, weapons of war are conflated with penises in more than one *double entendre*: 'Draw thy tool'; 'My naked weapon is out' (30, 32).

Another allusion in Juliet's wedding-night speech confirms in a quite different key the proximity of desire and death:

> Give me my Romeo, and when [he] shall die
> Take him and cut him out in little stars,
> And he will make the face of heaven so fine
> That all the world will be in love with night
> And pay no worship to the garish sun. (3.2.21–5)

There is some dispute about the pronoun in line 21. The earliest texts give 'I' but editors have generally supposed that 'he' makes more sense' 'when *he* shall die / Take *him*'. The editor of Arden 2 chooses 'I' in deference to the early texts. Pointing out that in the early modern period to *die* is to *come*, he sees the passage as alluding to simultaneous orgasm: 'like a rocket soaring up into the night sky and exploding into innumerable stars'. Arden 3 also gives 'I' and confirms this reading. They may be right, but to die is also to die. Kristeva opts for 'he' and argues that the passage shows 'Juliet's unconscious desire to break up Romeo's body'. Perhaps. My own view is that Juliet appeals for Romeo to be stellified: turned at his death into a constellation.

I am strengthened in this opinion by a moment in Chaucer's *House of Fame*, when the terrified Geoffrey, transported into the sky by a giant golden eagle, wonders whether Jove has it in mind to stellify him. Not yet, the eagle reassures him (2.584–99). Shakespeare was among Chaucer's greatest admirers. Geoffrey has in mind the stories attached to the constellations in classical mythology, and especially the myth of Ganymede. The beautiful boy snatched up by Jove himself in the form of an eagle to be his cupbearer and lover was immortalized as the constellation Aquarius. Orion, once a mighty hunter, was picked out in the night sky as a cluster of stars. As luck would have it, this was the fate Ben Jonson imagined for Shakespeare himself in the tribute he wrote for the Folio edition of the plays: 'I see thee in the hemisphere / Advanced, and made a constellation there.' Juliet appeals for Romeo to be perpetuated as a fretwork of stars that will outdo the sun in beauty. The preference is appropriate: for these lovers of the night it is darkness that excels. Misled soon afterwards by the Nurse's lamentations into thinking Romeo is dead already, she follows the same train of thought: 'Can heaven be so envious?' (3.2.40).

But however we choose to read the allusion to the stars, and whichever pronoun we prefer, the passage shows death as resident in the sexual imagining at the heart of the play. Indeed, the early modern pun indicates that the period took it to have a legitimate place there. And is it, after all, such a surprising thought? We take for granted its inclusion in the conjugal vow of fidelity 'till death us do part'. *Romeo and Juliet* shows the deadly element in love intensified by the pressure of the time: the feud leads to a secret marriage and Romeo's banishment, while the recklessness of desire is deepened by prohibition and urgency. What looks at first glance like an opposition between the lovers and their society turns out to be a parallel, as external violence both threatens and compounds the 'violent delights' (2.6.9) internal to love itself.

Writing matters

In view of all this, what can you say about the tomb scene itself? A good place to start would be the differences between Paris and Romeo as they approach the monument in 5.3: on the one hand, the publicly approved potential bridegroom and, on the other, the secret, outlawed, actual husband. There are obvious parallels: each comes with a torch and an attendant; each insists on being alone. But they have very different projects. What do they bring with them? How do they deal with their servants? What do they do?

How do you interpret the imagery of Romeo's long speech, only briefly interrupted by Balthasar, as he forces open the tomb (5.3.22–48)? Are there any surprises here? How does the vocabulary relate to the earlier speeches of the most poetic of all lovers, or the apparently 'effeminate' figure of the middle scenes of the play? And how does the utterance compare with the popular image of Romeo as a sentimental, moony youth? At the same time, for a playgoer (or a reader) who has been paying attention throughout, is there also a sense in which the speech brings together images of love and death that have already pervaded the play?

These are difficult questions about the most complex of issues. I might as well confess that I have found this chapter hard to write. What *exactly*, I have had to keep asking myself, is the point I'm making? If my understanding of the play doesn't exist in some unspecified form outside the words, why don't the words come easily? Is there, after all, a place of pure ideas beyond the signifier, analogous to the realms of pure love and pure grief that Juliet imagines? In the end, although it sometimes feels that way, I think not. When making sense of a difficult text, once I get past the stage of baffled incomprehension, what I experience is something like a doubt, an uncertainty, a resistance to the obvious reading, a riddle. The *idea* is the answer (or partial answer) to the riddle and it doesn't exist until I have found words that reveal it with a degree, at least, of clarity. Shakespeare is difficult, and it's not just the archaism of the language that makes him so. In addition, it's the way possible and sometimes contradictory meanings crowd into a small space, challenging us to specify the work they do. This is also, of course, what makes Shakespeare exciting: meanings collide and clash, creating a degree of exhilaration as, one after another, improbable conjunctions defy expectation. Without being Shakespeare, critics are not likely to do justice to the texts. Even so, we don't want to betray them. Our job is to use all the resources at our disposal, especially the historical *Oxford English Dictionary*, and to be as lucid as we can with respect to the material in front of us.

If the comparison between Paris and Romeo does not exhaust your energies, try Romeo's long final speech (5.3.74–120). (That will!) How does it engage an audience in experiencing this climactic moment? What range of topics does it include? How far is it sad, macabre, triumphant, all three? And does that combination of emotions perhaps have something to say about the nature of tragedy?

CHAPTER FOUR

Shakespeare retells the tale

Shakespeare at work

Ever since the end of the eighteenth century, when Romantic authors called poetry the spontaneous overflow of powerful feelings, we have liked to believe that imaginative writing springs mysteriously from an inner core of being, the personality of the author, in conjunction with his or her 'experience'. Creative writers themselves are often deeply attached to this idea, and critical biography does its best to trace the relationship between the life and feelings of a unique individual and the resulting texts, while tracking down the real-life originals of fictional events and characters.

Early modern culture, by contrast, imagined no such thing. Instead, the primary source of writing was other writing. No particular merit was attached to the invention of plots: there were plenty of good stories ready and waiting to be retold. The tale of Romeo and Juliet was already familiar; audiences could probably be relied on to relish another version of a sad but engaging love story.

If this seems odd, it is worth reflecting that our own practices are not, after all, so fundamentally different: we too seem to relish the same stories retold. By now, there cannot be many people in the Western world who are not already well-informed about the sexual lives of the Tudor monarchs, and yet Henry VIII and his wives, Elizabeth and her conjectural lovers, continue to furnish material for novels, plays and television series. Harry Potter films are addressed above all to Harry Potter readers, who want to see how the story will be reimagined for the screen. *Romeo and Juliet* itself has been much recycled since Shakespeare's time.

Recycling is more than repetition. The appeal is evidently not the newness of the plot but a novelty in the telling. Some bold works make cultural history by breaking radically with the conventions; others repeat them with minor variations. *Romeo and Juliet* reinscribes a well-known tale, but it does so with a difference that allows us access to its singularity. Arthur Brooke's *Romeus and Juliet* translates into English verse a French version of an Italian work by Matteo Bandello, who himself retold an existing story in prose. Brooke's poem was first printed in 1562, two years before Shakespeare was born, but it was reissued in 1587, within a decade of the first performance of the play. The events of *Romeo and Juliet* follow Brooke's version quite closely in some respects, so there is no doubt that Shakespeare knew it.

Meanwhile, in 1567 William Painter included a prose translation of the same French text in the second volume of his *Palace of Pleasure*, a collection of translated love stories that also included the source of *All's Well That Ends Well*. Volume 2, containing 'Romeo and Julietta' was reissued in 1580. Opinions vary on the relevance of Painter's version but, in my view, we can find enough verbal echoes to demonstrate its part in the composition of the tragedy. There is no indication that Shakespeare went back to the French or Italian versions.

And why is any of this of the slightest interest to anyone wanting to make sense of *Romeo and Juliet*? Stephen Greenblatt once called source-hunting the 'elephants' graveyard' of literary history, and certainly the practice can lead to dusty outcomes. But analysis of the way the play treats its sources is as close as we can get to seeing Shakespeare at work. In the rewriting, as well as in the conversion from narrative to drama, Shakespeare, perhaps in conjunction with the rest of the theatrical company, makes choices, selecting, expanding, deleting, reappropriating. Some of these choices concern the grand arc of the story, while others centre on minute textual details.

Torches revisited

Let's start small. The torches Juliet teaches to burn bright (1.5.43; see Chapter 2) play a different role in the sources, where it is *Romeo*'s good looks they illuminate. Both Brooke and Painter indicate that Romeo is the only Montague to go to the feast. He is putting himself through a self-imposed regime of attending parties in the hope of forgetting his first, unrequited love. Romeo turns up with his unnamed companions wearing a mask, but after supper the others all remove their visors. Embarrassed by the thought of exposure in a hostile environment, Romeo retreats to a corner, but his hopes of finding a dark place are doomed to disappointment. In Brooke, 'brighter than the sun, the waxen torches shone' (line 173) so that he is clearly visible to all, attracting the eyes of the women in particular 'To wonder at his sightly shape and beauty's spotless hue' (176). Since they are also impressed by his audacity in venturing into Capulet territory, Romeo now becomes a source of widespread female admiration.

Perhaps there is something faintly distasteful in the identification of the romantic hero as a sex-object for the whole of Verona. If so, it is compounded by the fact that Romeus in turn assesses each of the ladies present, until his eye alights on Juliet. She, in Brooke's account, is 'right fair, of perfect shape / Which Theseus or Paris would have chosen to their rape' (197–8). Here Brooke's allusions let him down: even if we acknowledge that the meaning of *rape* is closer to 'abduction' than the modern term allows, these are not auspicious comparisons. Theseus was notorious for his sexual rapacity; most infamously, he ran off with Ariadne and then abandoned her on the island of Naxos. Paris, meanwhile, left Greece with Helen, wife of Menelaus, thus giving rise to the Trojan War and the tragic destruction of the glory that was Troy.

Shakespeare opts to transfer the effect of the bright light to Romeo's first sight of Juliet, integrating the brilliance of the torches into his perception of a beauty that exceeds it. In Painter's tale Shakespeare would have found Romeo's beauty illuminated by 'the torches which burned very bright', a phrase closer to the words he chose, while Theseus and Paris are nowhere to be found. There is nothing distasteful in Shakespeare's Romeo, who is not looking for a new love but cannot, even so, restrain his admiration for Juliet: 'O, she doth teach the torches to burn bright'.

In technical terms, the dramatist has changed a metonymy to a metaphor. Metonymy invests a thing with the properties of an adjacent or contiguous object; it acts by a process of substitution or displacement. Whether deliberately or not, Brooke and Painter both allow their readers to associate the brightness of the torches with the beauty they illuminate: lights and hero, we are to understand, all shine. Shakespeare, who was nothing if not an astute reader, evidently perceives the parallel but condenses it into a metaphor that permits Juliet's beauty to outdo in Romeo's eyes the radiance that surrounds her. The effect of the change is thus doubly idealizing: first, what shines is nothing so specific as a 'shape' but a quality not otherwise defined; second, Juliet is compared favourably not with other women but with the flaming sources of light.

If the lovers are rarefied by this means, the element of worldly wisdom is not discarded but transferred to other figures in the play, most notably Mercutio but also the Nurse. She, too, is put together from hints in the sources. Painter's nurse is a good old woman who loves the girl she has nourished; Brooke's, by contrast, has to be bribed to help. Brooke's Romeus also pays the nurse well for her messages;

in consequence, she praises him highly to Juliet on her return. Brooke's nurse praises Paris, however, when the time comes; Romeus will surely never return but, if he does, Juliet will have the best of both worlds, a husband and a lover. In a combination of the caring old woman and the cynical, self-seeking servant, Shakespeare finds the makings of a developed comic figure. And Brooke supplies one more critical ingredient. His nurse is incurably garrulous and given to rhapsodic accounts of Juliet's infancy: '"A pretty babe", quod she, "it was when it was young; / Lord, how it could full prettily have prated with it tongue!"' (lines 653–4, cf. 2.5.192).

Unless Shakespeare had access to other versions of the story now lost, the tale of the child falling on her face is his invention, along with the toddler's innocent acquiescence in the old husband's sexual joke as retailed by the Nurse: 'Thou wilt fall backward when thou hast more wit' (1.3.43). By this means, the play prepares the way for the Nurse's praise of Paris, then Romeo, then Paris again, as occasion requires, in line with her dedication to 'happy nights' (1.3.106), whoever supplies them.

Tybalt's ghost

The economical habit of putting elements from one location to good use in another repeatedly influences details of the play. Painter's version shows the dying Romeo in the tomb placating an imagined ghost of Thibault. He is prompted to this by seeing the corpse of his victim and cousin by marriage next to Julietta's body in the vault. 'And if thy ghost do wish and cry out for vengeance upon me, what greater or more cruel satisfaction canst thou desire to have, or henceforth hope for, than to see him which murdered thee to be empoisoned with his own hands and buried by thy side?' Menacing ghosts had a long history in fireside tales, while their thirst for revenge featured in the plays of Seneca, appearing one by one in English translation during the 1560s. Shakespeare would draw on the motif in *Hamlet* and elsewhere. Brooke's Romeus appeals to Tybalt's 'restless sprite', wherever it may now be (line 2660) but his utterance is more diffuse, more open to the interpretation that the victim's soul, severed from the body in death, may be hovering somewhere near the carcase before its last journey to heaven or hell (cf. 3.1.128–9). *Sprites* (spirits) and *ghosts* were to a high degree interchangeable (it was Painter's Romeo who named Friar Lawrence 'my ghostly father' [cf. *Romeo and Juliet*, 2.3.41]); either of them might haunt the living. But a ghost that cries out for vengeance is more likely, by a whisker, to be a revenant uncannily back from the dead.

Shakespeare's Romeo also assures the dead Tybalt he is now appeased and asks his forgiveness (5.3.97–101). But the play deletes the ghost from these last moments, perhaps on the grounds that it distracts attention from the heroic love scene that culminates in Romeo's death. In the sources, the sequence is as follows: Romeo swallows the poison and dies slowly; he bids Juliet a last farewell; then he declares Tybalt duly avenged; finally, he casts himself on the mercy of God. Shakespeare cuts the appeal to God: suicide was an unforgiveable sin. He also curtails the address to Tybalt, and brings the focus of Romeo's long final speech back to Juliet, their last embrace, and 'engrossing death' (115).

But Tybalt's ghost does not go to waste. In the play it resurfaces in Juliet's terror as she swallows the Friar's potion. According to the sources, she vividly anticipates the horrors of waking in the tomb, perhaps among serpents and worms, until her appalled imagination conjures Tybalt's corpse and the surrounding bones and bodies, so that she gulps down the mixture, shaking with fear. But Shakespeare, who expands on the horrors, brings the speech to a climax in Tybalt's vengeful ghost, with the double effect of sustaining the anxiety and bringing attention back to the fight that caused their separation – and Romeo:

O, look, methinks I see my cousin's ghost
Seeking out Romeo that did spit his body
Upon a rapier's point. Stay, Tybalt, stay!
Romeo, Romeo, Romeo, here's drink. I drink to thee. (4.3.55–8)

Juliet's ghost

In the sources, both Romeo and Juliet make speeches as they die. Juliet's is so prolix that the Friar and Romeo's servant are obliged to leave her to it. At last she affirms that she will delay no longer, in case she cannot find Romeo's spirit among the dead. And so, she tells her lover, she

willingly offers to thee her ghost,
To th'end that no wight else but thou might have just cause to boast
Th'enjoying of my love, which aye I have reserved
Free from the rest, bound unto thee, that hast it well deserved;
That so our parted sprites from light that we see here,
In place of endless light and bliss may ever live y-fere. (lines 2783–8)

The effect is to offer a quasi-happy ending: unable to be 'y-fere' (together) on earth, the couple will live united in heaven. Whether coincidentally or not, Michael Boyd's production of the play for the Royal Shakespeare Company in 2000 showed the dead Romeo and Juliet silently emerge from the tomb as the families came together, and depart through the audience, unseen by all on stage but the Friar, who followed them off.

Needless to say, this interpretation gave rise to controversy. Such an ending is more romantic, less austere, than Shakespeare's version, where Juliet's final speech is terse, her death more or less instantaneous. Their union in an afterlife focuses audience attention on the lovers and distracts it from the community ultimately responsible for their tragedy.

From narrative to drama

That community, vividly realized in the play, is mainly Shakespeare's construction, as far as we know. In the sources, the rest of Verona effectively forms a backdrop to the story of the lovers. Its residents are brought on as needed by events, and invested with rudimentary characteristics, as required. The hostility between the households is indicated but not shown in action until the fight that leads Romeo to kill Tybalt; some young gentlemen are said to accompany Romeo to the Capulet feast, but they have no names and play no part in the action. Tybalt himself does not appear at the feast; Paris does not visit the tomb.

Perhaps it is here that the difference between narrative and drama is most apparent. In a story figures can come and go; on the stage actors need parts to play – theatres have their own economy. The consensus is that Shakespeare's company usually included about 15 actors, eight of them 'sharers', or partners in the venture, and the rest hired players and boys with varying degrees of training. Conjecturally, and depending on how we choose to count them, *Romeo and Juliet* includes six or seven substantial male parts (Romeo, Mercutio, Tybalt, Paris, Capulet, the Friar and Benvolio). There is no reliable evidence on whether the Nurse was played by a boy or an adult, perhaps an older boy. In addition, there are three parts for experienced boys, Juliet's very demanding. (We know that one of the sharers, the clown Will Kemp, played the Nurse's servant, Peter.) Shakespeare, an actor himself, who worked in the theatre every day, would know that his play had better give its main actors work to do, and in the unlikely event that he forgot this, the company was there to remind him. While in the sources Paris does not appear until after

Romeo's banishment, Shakespeare introduces him as a suitor (1.2) before Romeo appears. He is invited to the feast and is presumably there among the 'Guests' mentioned in the stage direction (1.5.15SD). Paris returns in 3.4 when Capulet names the day, and then visits the Friar to make the arrangements, meeting the tearful Juliet as she comes for counsel (4.1.). He arrives to collect his bride in 4.5 and visits her tomb in 5.3. His recurring presence builds not only a role but the dramatic tension – Juliet's choice is at odds with her parents' from the beginning.

Narrative can afford to be vague about what happened. Romeo's effrontery in attending the feast, for example, is registered by the sources in the attention of the ladies, who marvel that he dares to be there. For some reason, the sources continue, the Capulets did nothing: perhaps they didn't want to upset the other guests; maybe they thought he was too young to constitute a suitable target for indignation; possibly they feared the wrath of the Prince. And Brooke adds frankly, 'the cause I do not know' (line 184). Shakespeare fills the space this uncertainty makes available. His Tybalt and Capulet have already established their positions in the opening scene, one young and the inveterate enemy of all Montagues, the other old and kindly – so far. Tybalt's outburst in the party scene dramatizes the outrage of youth and the relative benevolence of the old man, while establishing the command of the master of a household over his junior relations. This same power will be tragically exercised in due course by a father no longer ready to indulge his daughter.

The feud

The episode also integrates the hostility between the households into the love story. It is while Romeo gazes at the figure who teaches the torches to burn bright that Shakespeare's Tybalt sends for his rapier. This feud is more than the setting for a story of unhappy love. Instead, it constitutes a deadly tear in the social fabric that threatens to part the lovers from the moment they meet. From now on it is evident that if Paris doesn't separate them, Tybalt surely will.

While the sources mention the discord at the beginning, the tragedy shows it. Shakespeare opens the play with a confrontation, and not only between the principals. Violent action is likely to secure the attention of daylight playgoers less disciplined than our own theatre audiences. Fencing matches were a familiar source of entertainment in the period and spectators had the right to expect a high degree of skill in the stage fights. At the same time, the theatrical spectacle registers the nature of the conflict. That the servants are infected shows how deep the enmity goes; the pointless insults designed to motivate a brawl show that the cause, if ever there was one, has been forgotten. While the participation of the citizens in eager support of one side or the other demonstrates the implications for a whole society of antagonism between its prominent members, the efforts of the old men to recover their lost aggressive youth throw into relief its folly.

The Prince's intervention represents the state's attempt to impose law on an anarchic community. His summons to 'our common judgement-place' (1.1.100) would have had a topical resonance for an early modern audience. The Tudor monarchs had tried, with varying degrees of conviction and success, to weld warring medieval households into a single nation, subjecting private quarrels to the arbitration of the courts. The inter-familial Wars of the Roses, kept alive in memory by contemporary historians, as well as by Shakespeare's own history plays, were depicted as grim struggles for power in high places, ultimately against the interests of the protagonists themselves, as well as the people. Meanwhile, at the time of the play, brawls continued on the London streets. Elizabethan aristocrats away from their estates remained intensely quarrelsome, and their duelling set a poor example to the London populace, whose response to the poverty induced by a rapidly expanding city and equally rapidly rising food prices was understandably violent. There were major riots in June 1595, when famine prompted insurrection and the harsh punishments meted out by the City incited further conflict.

In the play everyone seems to have access to a weapon – even Juliet carries a knife (4.1.54, 62; 4.3.23). The options are established from the opening scene. Benvolio's failed attempt to keep the peace and Tybalt's relentless belligerence anticipate Romeo's later inability to pacify his new cousin. Benvolio ('good will') is Shakespeare's creation on the basis of an anonymous friend in the sources. The equally peaceable effort of the Friar to unite the households through their children (2.3.87–8) is more than incidental. It promotes what is literally a more civil-ized way forward for 'civil hands' than the waste of 'civil blood' (Prologue, 4).

The statues

The golden statues also appear to be Shakespeare's invention. In Painter the families are reconciled in tears, while the Prince orders a marble column to commemorate the grave of the lovers. Brooke allots them a grand tomb on marble pillars but it is not clear who commissions it. What Shakespeare makes of this is worth quoting in full:

Cap. O brother Montague, give me thy hand.
This is my daughter's jointure, for no more
Can I demand.
Mont. But I can give thee more,
For I will raise her statue in pure gold,
That whiles Verona by that name is known,
There shall no figure at such rate be set
As that of true and faithful Juliet.
Cap. As rich shall Romeo's by his lady's lie,
Poor sacrifices of our enmity. (5.3.296–304)

After all the rhetoric a simple offer of reconciliation, but one that has the power to repair the city. While the bridegroom's family traditionally brought a financial jointure to the marriage, Capulet will confine his requirement to joined hands. Montague will more than fulfil the conventional obligation, however, with gold. But this is not to be gold as hard cash; instead, he promises a work of art that will memorialize Juliet's fidelity and, by implication, her worth and beauty. As long as the city lasts, an image of the figure who taught the torches to burn bright will shine in gold as a symbol of unity.

What can Capulet do but reciprocate the promise? Romeo's golden image will lie by Juliet's. *Statue* included what we mean by the word, or a picture, or an effigy. The Reformation had largely removed the vertical statues of saints from their niches, and the classical custom of honouring heroes in stone had not yet established itself in England. Tomb sculpture, however, was a major art form at this time; its products, in stone or alabaster, are still to be found in parish churches and cathedrals in the UK, vindicating the claim to durability. While merchant and gentry couples were commonly represented facing each other as they knelt in prayer, noble husbands and wives lay side by side in fine dress, richly painted. Where most editors emend the 1599 text's 'I will ray her statue in pure gold' in line with the 1623 Folio's 'raise', 'ray' (array) makes sense: Montague will gild Juliet's effigy. Either way, the horizontal figures of Romeo and Juliet, moulded or decorated in pure gold, exceed the norm to represent a work of art that perhaps only art could conceive.

Their commemoration as tomb sculptures lying side by side proclaims in a single image the marriage and the deaths of the protagonists; the immortalization of their love does not cancel mourning for their loss. Meanwhile, the financial origin of the gold in the omitted marriage settlement is not forgotten: the 'rate' at which Juliet's effigy will be set is at once a worth and a cost; Romeo's statue will be 'as rich', as glorious and as expensive. The ambiguities echo Romeo's first reaction to the lady whose name he does not yet know: 'Beauty too rich for use, for earth too dear' (1.5.46). But now the price paid explicitly includes death, while the beneficiary is Verona, the city that arbitrarily, anarchically threw away such precious lives. These monuments are to serve as a reminder of the sacrifices civil conflict demands.

Disobedient children

The Prince ends with a promise of justice: 'Some shall be pardoned, and some punished' (5.3.308). He has already recognized that everyone has suffered by the feud, including himself (295), and now his final pronouncement offers playgoers a general sense of resolution and closure. Brooke and Painter, however, are more specific: they record the Apothecary hanged for selling poison; the Friar is set at liberty but opts to spend his remaining years as a hermit; the Nurse is banished for concealing a marriage. The play's deletion of this list of penalties has the effect of foregrounding the twin issues of true love and civil strife.

But the insistence in the sources on crime and punishment throws into relief a moral ambivalence in the culture that immediately preceded Shakespeare's. Was the earlier version a tale of love or a warning against vice? Did the deaths of Romeo and Juliet represent the sad fate of passion or the just consequence of defying the family? Brooke, it seems, could not make up his mind. The sympathetic story he tells is strangely at odds with the severe tone of his preface 'To the Reader'. Narratives, he tells us there, provide moral examples; they show what readers should emulate and what they should shun; his own is no exception:

> And to this end, good Reader, is this tragical matter written, to describe unto thee a couple of unfortunate lovers, thralling themselves to unhonest desire; neglecting

> the authority and advice of parents and friends; conferring their principal counsels with drunken gossips and superstitious friars (the naturally fit instruments of unchastity); attempting all adventures of peril for th' attaining of their wished lust; using auricular confession the key of whoredom and treason, for furtherance of their purpose; abusing the honourable name of lawful marriage to cloak the shame of stolen contracts; finally by all means of unhonest life hasting to most unhappy death.

The anti-Catholicism of Reformation values is clearly at work here: 'superstitious' friars are the engines of illicit sex; confession fosters not only fornication but also treason, since allegiance to a foreign pope threatens loyalty to the English queen. It is not entirely clear who the drunken gossips are – probably the Nurse. But the value most prominently contravened is marriage and the proper authority of parents in ordering it.

Was this what Brooke himself believed? Or was it, rather, what he thought might help to sell his poem? We have no way of knowing. But he himself mentions a play that recently set the same argument forth on the stage, eliciting great commendation. No such drama has ever been traced. Coincidentally or not, however, among the handful of plays that have survived from the era of Brooke's poem, more than one shows undisciplined children coming to a bad end. Thomas Ingelend's *Disobedient Child* centres on a young man who wilfully refuses to train for a profession when his father fails to insist on it. Instead, he marries young without parental consent and, once his funds are exhausted, the pleasures of the honeymoon give way to domestic violence. The love scenes are less than lyrical and the play is otherwise most notable for the comic exchanges between Blanch and Longtongue, the cooks who prepare the wedding feast in an episode that foreshadows the brief appearance of Potpan and his fellows as they make ready the Capulet party (*Romeo and Juliet*, 1.5.1–15). Evidently, the upstairs-downstairs theme has a long pedigree on the English stage.

Setting *The Disobedient Child* alongside the more or less contemporary *Romeus and Juliet* complicates our view of the past. It often seems that previous societies are more unified than our own, or that only contemporary culture is radically divided on the questions of the day. The early modern world contradicts this view. While popular romances were praising youthful love and fidelity, while Italian tales filtering into English culture were endorsing a more worldly understanding of desire, Reformation orthodoxy favoured the strict enforcement of rigorous parental control. At different moments Brooke's work embraces all three points of view.

That was in the 1560s. By the 1590s, when Shakespeare composed *Romeo and Juliet*, even if a sense of recklessness runs through the depiction of the lovers' 'violent delights' (2.6.9), young love had broadly won out against parental authority, at least in fiction. The reissue of Brooke's poem in 1587 retained the moralizing preface, but the title page now promoted the story as 'a rare example of true constancy'. Protestant Reformers had realized that if unmarried Catholic priests, friars and monks were to remain the butt of scorn, marriage had better be seen as a worthy alternative to celibacy. Love for a partner under the aegis of the church, they concluded, was an excellent way of imitating the love of God, while the caring heterosexual couple could be relied on to bring up their children as disciplined members of society. (Does this begin to sound familiar?) A spate of self-help manuals gave advice on how to ensure a happy and virtuous family life. The modern Western world had arrived, at least in theory.

If the Reformers now generally sided with love, they also hoped the parents could be persuaded to give their consent in the interests of harmony, and counselled the young to seek their approval. Meanwhile, however, in the upper reaches of society, where alliances involved the transfer of land and property, arranged marriages would continue to be the norm in practice for many years to come. *Romeo and Juliet* belongs to a moment when the understanding of marriage was in the balance. Her father calls Juliet a 'disobedient wretch' (3.5.160); on the other hand, by now she has no choice but to defy him. In Thomas Ingelend's play, it is the baffled father who invites pity from playgoers; in Shakespeare's, sympathy switches to the children. No doubt the popularity of *Romeo and Juliet* itself helped to tip the scales in favour of consent on the basis of romantic love.

Time scale

These days the prevailing criterion of value among critics, actors and directors alike, is realism. Despite the best efforts of modernism, notwithstanding the diversity of the literary curriculum, truth to life remains highly prized. Shakespeare is also highly prized; it therefore follows, so we are to believe, that the plays must be treated as realist. Verse is increasingly pronounced as prose: the beat of Shakespeare's rhythms, crucial, some would say, to the emotions they define, is disappearing from the theatre and dismissed as incongruous from the intimacy of film and television. Productions are increasingly staged in modern dress. The project is to bring Shakespeare as close as possible to soap opera, presumably on the assumption that this will make him more accessible.

This realist criterion generally remains unspoken, of course. Once spelt out, it would show itself to be absurd. Two actual teenagers who met at a party on Sunday evening, married in secret on Monday, parted early on Tuesday morning and killed themselves for love on Thursday, all the while addressing each other in blank verse, would surely go down in history, if at all, as deranged rather than iconic.

In practice, Shakespeare has opted to increase the improbability by speeding up the time scheme. In Bandello's Italian prose (and much more prosaic, not to say realistic) original, the lovers meet just after Christmas and die in September. The Italian Romeo has time to establish himself in Mantua; Juliet writes to him of the threatened marriage; he promises to come for her – and doesn't. Shakespeare's English sources faithfully reproduce the dates, and the narrative unfolds in a suitably leisurely way: for a week or two after the party Romeo and Juliet do no more than glimpse each other at a distance, before the hero finds his way to her garden. Their secret marriage continues for two or three months until Romeo kills Tybalt; Romeo spends several months in Mantua trying to get his exile repealed. By contrast, Shakespeare integrates the feud closely with the love story and its implications. It is as Romeo and Juliet first meet that Tybalt threatens violence; between their wedding and its consummation Romeo kills Tybalt and is sentenced to banishment; on the morning of Romeo's enforced departure, Juliet faces marriage to Paris.

The effect of this new time scale is to intensify both the passion between the lovers and the awareness of its tragic impossibility. This is idealizing, heroic, poetic *fiction*, not life. Does it follow that the play has nothing to say to us that matters? On the contrary. Raised above the level of banality, differentiated from the inarticulateness of everyday exchange, heightened *as* poetry, desire is made to live, rendered sympathetic and intelligible, permitted to display the reckless cross-currents of love and death that constitute passion.

Meanwhile, as I write, gang warfare, turf conflicts and sectarian violence continue to escape the best efforts of the law to guarantee the peaceful coexistence of innocent citizens; a couple have been found guilty of murder in the UK because they could not tolerate their 17-year-old daughter's longing for self-determination; the government is considering legislation against forced marriages. The issues that *Romeo and Juliet* puts before us (heroically, tragically, poetically) are not confined to the past.

Plays, in other words, can comment on important and continuing questions without any requirement to simulate the outward appearance of daily life. Realism is not the only option: there is more than one way to tell a story.

Writing matters

Leaving what some would think the best till last, we now come to Mercutio and your assignment. Mercutio is very incidental in the sources and is mostly Shakespeare's (or the company's) creation. The question that arises, then, is how his role contributes to the play as we have it. Perhaps unusually, it is possible to imagine a tragedy resembling the one we have but without Mercutio: his role seems in certain respects detachable. What, then, is the effect of his inclusion?

Here are some prompts. Not many people know that Mercutio began life in the Italian stories as Marcuccio the Squint-eyed, and his only other notable attributes were a way with women and very cold hands. The French translation deleted the squint, so this did not make its way into the English sources. But the hands did. At the feast Romeo and Juliet have so far exchanged no more than lingering glances. After Juliet excels in one of the dances, Romeo follows her to her seat next to 'another gentleman called Mercutio, which was a court-like gentleman, very well beloved of all men and by reason of his pleasant and courteous behaviour was in all companies well entertained'. Brooke's poem and Painter's prose narrative both follow the French source closely here. Mercutio, 'that was of audacity among maidens as a lion is among lambs', seized Juliet's hand in his, which was 'so cold both in winter and summer as the mountain ice'. Seeing this, Romeo instantly takes hold of her other hand, eliciting a response from Juliet: '"Blessed be the hour of your near approach"', she exclaims, but then love makes her tongue-tied. Overjoyed by this welcome, Romeo encourages her to explain, and she eventually summons the courage to confide that, where Mercutio has frozen her hand, Romeo has warmed it. At this, Romeo promises to serve her in any other way he can, and declares that the warmth of his hand is nothing to the fire of her eyes.

And that is the sum total of Mercutio's role in Shakespeare's English sources. How much of it survives in the play? Mercutio's courtesy and court-like behaviour, perhaps (he is closely related to the Prince [3.1.111]), but not the sexual predatoriness (he is not in any sense Romeo's rival). Nor does he act as an intermediary between the lovers: his cold hand as a prompt for conversation between them has vanished. But Romeo's hand has not disappeared: 'The measure done, I'll watch her place of stand / And, touching hers, make blessed my rude hand' (1.5.49–50). If you carried out the suggested analysis at the end of Chapter 2, you will know already what this leads to: the conventional banalities of the sources give way to a spirited exchange about hands that is at once romantic and witty. No one is tongue-tied (1.5.92–109).

Neither a Capulet nor a Montague, Mercutio is Romeo's friend. His wit and exuberance epitomize the male group, teasing and variously quarrelsome, that the play juxtaposes with the intimate, intense world of the lovers. Mercutio is entitled to mock Romeo, who is both a member of this group and, as a lover, apart from it. It is as a friend that Mercutio feels in honour bound to fight Tybalt when Romeo seems to back away from the challenge; it is also as a friend that Romeo feels compelled to avenge Mercutio's death, the outcome of his own calamitous intervention (3.1.124–31). In the sources, Romeo simply kills Tybalt in self-defence. What are the implications of the play's introduction of Mercutio into their fight?

Mercutio is responsible for much of the prose in the play, putting paid to the old view that the difference between prose and verse is a matter of class. Poetry heightens; prose is more casual, relaxed, comic or dismissive – in general. That is not to say that prose lacks pattern or form; it may be as artful as verse, even if the art lies in concealing its artfulness. Find examples of Mercutio's well-crafted prose (there are plenty in 2.4) and then reflect on his dying speech (3.1.97–105). What response does this succession of apparent understatements invite from playgoers?

If Mercutio is a master of prose, he is also responsible for some of the most fantastical poetry in the play (1.4.53–95). The Queen Mab speech has largely baffled source-hunters; it seems to come largely from Shakespeare's imagination (with possibly a sidelong glance at *The Terrors of the Night*, published in 1594 by the equally sceptical Thomas Nashe). Even such tiny fairies are not characteristic of English folklore, although they are also to be found in the contemporary *A Midsummer Night's Dream*. This is clearly a set piece: it freezes the action of the play and it adds nothing to the plot, unless we see it as emphasizing the isolation of the perturbed lover, Romeo, from his peer group, still carefree enough to indulge in witty make-believe.

Does it add anything to the *play* (apart from 40 lines of verse)? That is a hard question and one to which there is no orthodox answer. Thoughts you might be inclined to follow up, however, would include fanciful satire as a foil for tragic passion, the extension of the community to include the aspirations of social types not otherwise mentioned in the play, and the identification 300 years before Freud of dreams with the fulfilment of wishes in a realm not subject to rational control. Is the Queen Mab speech yet another case where fiction, in this instance the purest fantasy, can comment on life in a way closed to realism?

And finally, what do you make of the apparently incidental allusion to Mercutio at 5.3.75?

CHAPTER FIVE

Textual choices

The texts

Here is the first-ever printed representation of the heroine's death in *Romeo and Juliet*. Paris's page had run off when he saw his master fighting with Romeo in order to fetch the Watch, the nearest thing in Elizabethan England to the police. Hearing their approach in such compromising circumstances, the Friar has fled, but Juliet refuses to leave the tomb.

Enter watch.

Watch: This way, this way.
Jul: Aye, noise? Then must I be resolute.
O happy dagger thou shalt end my fear,
Rest in my bosom, thus I come to thee.
She stabs herself and falls.

I have modernized the spelling but changed nothing else, leaving the punctuation as it is given in the original text. If you know the play well, or if you check with your edition (5.3.169–70), this may not look entirely familiar.

The printed version of *An Excellent Conceited Tragedy of Romeo and Juliet* appeared in 1597, one or two years after the likely first performance of the play, in a single quarto volume about as big as a large modern paperback (Q1). ('Quarto' indicates the size of the book by reference to the number of pages produced when folding one large sheet of paper in the printing process. A quarto book consisted of sheets folded twice to produce four smaller leaves printed on both sides [eight pages].) The publishers promoted their work on the title page by appealing to the play's theatrical success: 'As it hath been often (with great applause) played publicly, by the right honourable the Lord of Hunsdon his servants.' There is no mystery about Lord Hunsdon. If theatrical companies derived their income from their audiences, their official authority depended on the patronage of a named member of the nobility. Lord Hunsdon was briefly the patron of the Shakespeare company in 1596–7.

Whether we can trust the claim to great applause depends on how we judge the accuracy of advertising, but there seems no good reason to doubt it. Early modern audiences had never seen anything quite like this before; surely they loved the way the story unfolded? In 1598 the dramatist Henry Porter was the first of several to borrow elements of the plot and parody the dialogue of Shakespeare's play in his comedy *Two Angry Women of Abington* for the rival company at the Rose theatre. As further evidence of the play's popularity, two more quarto editions would be published before it was included in the Folio of 1623, the collection of plays published as a tribute to Shakespeare by his fellow actors at the Globe, along with Q4, now ascribed to the same year as the Folio. (A folio volume is large and impressive, its size determined by folding the large sheet only once to make two leaves [four pages].) The first time the play appeared, however, in 1597, the title indicates a print-shop assumption that the audience also relished the conceits: the wit, density and inventiveness of the language. Shakespeare is not mentioned.

Two years later, when a second quarto volume appeared from the workshop of a different printer, Juliet's death scene has changed:

Enter Boy and Watch.

Watch. Lead boy, which way.

Juli. Yea, noise? then I'll be brief. O happy dagger
This is thy sheath, there rust and let me die.

There is no stage direction here.

Presented, as we so often are, with seamless modern editions of Shakespeare's work, it would be easy to assume that the plays miraculously formed themselves into immortal words, to travel from the dramatist's domed head through the quill pen depicted on his monument in Stratford-upon-Avon and onto the page we have in front of us. If only. In practice, along with at least seventeen other plays attributed to Shakespeare, *Romeo and Juliet* exists in more than one early modern version, each asserting a right to our attention, so that in the process of establishing a single edition for performance or interpretation, editors have to make choices.

How does this second quarto (Q2) of 1599 affirm its authority? Once again, the title page naturally invokes the play's excellence. The conceits are no longer mentioned (although, paradoxically, in this version there are more of them) and nor is the applause. But Q2 claims to have been rectified, expanded and improved: *The Most Excellent and Lamentable Tragedy of Romeo and Juliet. Newly corrected, augmented, and amended:* As it hath been sundry times publicly acted, by the Right Honourable the Lord Chamberlain his servants. The Lord Chamberlain had now resumed his patronage of the Shakespeare company, to retain it until 1603, when they became the King's Men. Once again, the dramatist is not mentioned; presumably, his name was not quite yet the selling point it would become, although quartos of other plays show that that process was under way by 1598.

The claim to augmentation is vindicated. Q2 is longer than Q1 by more than one-fifth. Some of our favourite passages, the most lyrical exchanges between the lovers among them, appear only in Q2. Sometimes, but not always, Q2 makes better sense. Yet how far should we rely on the assertion that this is the corrected, and therefore by implication authoritative, version? Many editors have taken the title page at face value as justifying a preference for Q2. Traditionally, this was seen as the 'good' text and the proper basis of all modern editions. Here is Brian Gibbons, editor of Arden 2 (1980), on the opening page of his introduction, defending Q2 against its predecessor:

> The statement that Q2 is 'newly corrected, augmented, and amended' means that it is a replacement of the first edition, not a revision of an earlier version of the play. *Romeo and Juliet* Q1 is a Bad Quarto, piratical and dependent on an especially unreliable means of transmission for the text ... The Bad Quarto of *Romeo and Juliet* provoked the publication of a Good Quarto a couple of years later.

Well, that sounds decisive. But notice that the case for the goodness of Q2 and the corresponding badness of Q1 depends in the first instance on a title page designed to sell copies. Call me sceptical but I'm not sure that invoking a sales pitch to enlist one text against another by analogy with sheep and goats is the most reliable way forward. 'Corrected' might be read as supporting the Gibbons case that Q2 was issued to replace an inadequate Q1, but what about 'amended'? Might that not suggest precisely the 'revision' he repudiates? Moreover, Gibbons was not always quite so resolute on behalf of Q2 in editorial practice.

We shall come back to this story of 'good' and 'bad' quartos in due course, but first let's see what *we* think about Juliet's death scene. What exactly is the difference between Q1 and Q2? At the level of plot, not much: the Watch arrives, Juliet hears them, plunges Romeo's dagger into her body and dies. But in textual detail there are elements to support Q2's claim to correctness, or at least greater precision. For example, the Q1 Watch bustles on assertively – they seem to know exactly where they're going: 'This way, this way.' The Q2 Watch is less confident, and appeals to the Page for directions. This has the advantage of reminding the audience that they're there on his summons.

Juliet's first line in Q1 makes perfectly good sense: 'Aye, noise? Then must I be resolute.' The affirmative refers back to the Friar's claim to have heard sounds, and resolution is exactly the quality the occasion calls for. Since there is no poison left over, she must die by violence. But the line doesn't scan. An iambic pentameter calls for five stressed syllables – as in Q2: 'Yea noise? then I'll be brief. O happy dagger'. (Say it out loud and beat time if you don't believe me.) Moreover, 'brief' is exactly what she is: after Romeo's long dying speech (considerably longer in Q2 than it is in Q1) Juliet's death scene is terse to the point of minimalism. A less competent dramatist might cover the rhetorical ground a second time with the heroine but this play doesn't repeat itself at the critical moment. So far, Q2 seems to have the advantage, as most modern editors recognize.

But then we come to questions of taste. Here is Q1 again: 'O happy dagger thou shalt end my fear, / Rest in my bosom, thus I come to thee.' This scans. It also makes sense: Romeo's dagger (happy to have belonged to him, perhaps, luckily available, and privileged to have a role now) will put an end to Juliet's fear – of the tomb itself or, more likely, of prevention by the Watch from taking the action that will enable her to join her dead lover. And the concept is perfectly 'Shakespearean': 'Husband, I come!', exclaims Cleopatra, as she kills herself to follow the dead Antony (*Antony and Cleopatra*, 5.2.285). The invocation of death as 'rest' echoes Romeo's own promise to set up his 'everlasting rest' here with Juliet (5.3.110).

And yet most editors have preferred to start with Q2: 'O happy dagger / This is thy sheath, there rust and let me die'. Both texts will later indicate that Juliet takes the dagger from its sheath at Romeo's back, where it has no further use, to be 'mis-sheathed' (Q2) or 'sheathed' (Q1) in her own heart (5.3.203–5). Q2 is therefore more consistent – or more repetitive, depending on your point of view. Q2 is bleaker: there is no confirmation of the projected rest. Perhaps that refusal of consolation appeals to modern tastes? If so, however, that is no guarantee that it pleased Elizabethan audiences better.

Meanwhile, the choice between 'rest' and 'rust' has in its time aroused strong feelings. Nowhere is the case against 'rust' stated more forcefully than in the New Shakespeare version edited by John Dover Wilson and G. I. Duthie in 1955: 'Q2 "rust" ... makes sense of a kind, but one hideously unpoetical, and literally preposterous with "and let me die" following, while "rest" accords with "happy" and the consummation she craves.' This edition follows Q2 but replaces 'rust' with 'rest' from Q1. The accompanying note adds that 'a dagger naturally rests, rather than rusts, in its sheath'.

Fair enough: a sheath wouldn't be much use if it allowed the weapon to crumble away. 'Unpoetical', 'preposterous': is it, then, blind commitment to the 'good' Q2 that justifies the preference for 'rust' in so many more recent editions? Not necessarily. This new and unsuitable 'sheath' is no longer there to protect the instrument; instead, the idea of the iron rusting in Juliet's flesh is macabre in a play that increasingly emphasizes the Gothic. The word invokes the decay of this world, 'where moth and rust doth corrupt' (Matthew 6, 19) and where, by implication, feuds destroy innocent love. In its shock value, the image reiterates the notion of death as a lover taking possession of Juliet's body, but this time, since the penetration is effected by Romeo's dagger, death and the dead husband are no longer in competition with one another. Juliet goes to join them both; for her the dead Romeo has become synonymous with death itself. More relaxed, now, with modernism than Dover Wilson and his colleagues must have been, we are more ready to take the 'preposterous' in our stride, and relish what is 'unpoetical' in poetry. 'Rust' is daring (Shakespearean, then?) where 'rest' is conventional.

As you see, I like 'rust'. But I am also aware that my preference might well be the effect of my own postmodern location. I like to think that the image speaks across four centuries from one violent, disrupted and intensely inventive moment to another, but I'm not sure I can assert with any authority that Shakespeare shared my judgement. This tiny instance exemplifies the kinds of choices editors are repeatedly obliged to make in the construction of a single *Romeo and Juliet*.

And then there's the stage direction: 'She stabs herself and falls.' Almost all editors, however resolutely they defend Q2, borrow this, which appears only in Q1: it seals the exact moment of Juliet's death, only implicit in Q2 and therefore open to interpretation. Evidently, Q1 is not all 'bad'.

Q1: The case for

Indeed, it isn't. The first quarto is exceptionally rich in stage directions and, if we trust it, may give clues to performance in early productions. For example, in the scene where Mercutio teases the Nurse, only Q1 reveals that the cheeky tormentor's 'old hare hoar [or whore]' is delivered while '*He walks by them, and sings*' (2.4.129SD), for all the world as if his insult had no relevance to the present moment. A few lines later the Nurse, infuriated by the jokes at her expense but unable to retaliate adequately, vents her wrath on her servant as, according to Q1, '*She turns to Peter her man*' (148SD). Perhaps revealingly, when the protagonist arrives to be married at the Friar's cell, Q1 gives '*Enter Juliet somewhat fast, and embraceth Romeo*' (2.6.15SD). The contradictory moment when the Nurse returns with both the rope ladder that will bring the newly-weds together and the report of Tybalt's death that will part them again, is briefly indicated in Q2: '*Enter Nurse with cords*'. Q1, more graphic, captures the paradox visually: '*Enter Nurse wringing her hands, with the ladder of cords in her lap*' (3.2.31SD). When the Nurse counsels compliance with the marriage to Paris and thus leaves Juliet isolated, Q1 notes that the heroine glares at her departing back, '*She looks after Nurse*', as she condemns her counsel: 'Ancient damnation!' (3.5.236). And in one key instance, Q1 might explain what is less clear in Q2. If Paris is ready to cut his losses, no wonder her anxious father gets heavy with Juliet. When in 3.4 Capulet explains to the Count that his daughter won't be down again tonight, Q1 is less elaborate than Q2. In the first,

> *Paris:* These times of woe afford no time to woo,
> Madam farewell, commend me to your daughter.
> *Paris offers to go in, and Capulet calls him again.*
> *Cap:* Sir Paris? I'll make a desperate tender of my child.
> I think she will be ruled in all respects by me.

And Capulet goes straight on to set the date. Lady Capulet's intervention in Q2 leaves the sudden switch to authoritarianism less readily explicable (10–11).

In modern editions, often replete with stage directions, these contributions from the first printed text may not seem like much. But the indications of staging in early modern plays are few and far between, sometimes confined to exits and entrances, and not always reliable even on that issue. I worry about the scattering of editorial stage directions in modern editions of the plays: sometimes they point only to what is implied by the words; sometimes, with the best intentions, they owe more to the assumptions of the editor and can mislead. A good edition generally indicates modern interpolations typographically.

Where early modern stage directions do appear, on the other hand, they can offer major clues to the way things were done. Theatre is visual as well as verbal: much of what we can learn about how performances looked in Shakespeare's own time comes from the original stage directions. When Juliet drinks the potion in 4.3, we owe to Q1 the information that '*She falls upon her bed within the curtains*'. Possibly this refers to the curtained 'discovery space' at the back of the stage; more likely, it indicates a four-poster with bed-hangings, easily wheeled on and off the stage. In the next scene, when the entire company assemble to lead the bride to church, only to find her, as they think, dead, Q1 notes that '*All at once cry out and wring their hands*'. And in Q1 the stage direction offers this whole episode a kind of closure: '*They all but the Nurse go forth, casting rosemary on her and shutting the curtains.*'

Stories of pirates

Despite the number of subsequent editions published in Shakespeare's lifetime and just beyond, we can afford to concentrate our attention mostly on the differences between the first two. Q3 was derived from Q2; the Folio of 1623 was derived from Q3; Q4 was printed from Q3, though it also took account of Q1. Most modern editors, setting out to form a single version of the play, and basing their text on the longer, more lyrical Q2, nonetheless incorporate many of the stage directions from Q1. Brian Gibbons, who so condemned the first quarto as 'bad' and 'piratical', takes over most of the stage directions from the despised version.

This was not as illogical as it might seem. For much of the twentieth century, a story had progressively taken hold concerning the piracy Gibbons ascribes to the production of the 'bad' quartos in general. With individual variations, this ran roughly as follows. The playhouse scripts were precious to the company; publication in print would diminish their control over their own material, which was carefully guarded. However, the same scripts were also precious to unscrupulous printing shops, which stood to make money by putting them on the market. The question was how they were to get hold of the copy. Scholarly speculation eventually came to settle on the theory that an actor or actors from the play would sell what they could remember of the text, and make up the rest, to supplement their own incomes. This process of 'memorial reconstruction' explained the badness of the 'bad' quartos; where these resembled the 'good' quartos, the putative pirates had remembered accurately, perhaps because these were their very own lines, or at least because they had been onstage in the scene in question. Where the first quarto differed radically from the 'good' second one, the actors, who were not given complete written copies of the plays but only their own speeches and cues, were probably in the green room or tiring house and 'reconstructed' as best they could. On the basis of this story, a good deal of scholarly energy was expended on determining which parts had been played by the actors who had sold the company's birthright for a handful of silver. Candidates in *Romeo and Juliet* have included Romeo himself, as well as Paris, and possibly Mercutio. 'Bad' quartos were not just textually inadequate; they were also morally reprobate. The company, appalled by the pitiful version of the play ascribed to it, had no choice but to issue a 'good', correct version, exactly as it had flowed from the dramatist's pen.

Q1: The case for resumed

No wonder, then, that Q1 could be counted on for stage directions; according to this story, it was relayed to the printer by the very actors who had carried out some of them. But astute readers will have noticed another possibility here. If Q1 was allowed some authority on the grounds invented by scholars to explain its existence, perhaps it could be trusted now and then to get the words right too? Actors, if they were the source, might not always misremember. Let's examine some instances. These are all minor cases: what is at stake for the moment is not a radical rewriting of the play we know, but a choice between two versions – with the project of disrupting the old, grand, binary opposition between authorial integrity in Q2 and thespian piracy in Q1.

Here, for example, is Romeo in love. Q1 gives: 'Why then, O brawling love, O loving hate, / O any thing, of nothing first create!' (1.1.174–5). Q2 reproduces this but with a change to 'created'. 'Created' modernizes an archaic form, still common in Shakespeare's early plays but in the process of changing in the course of his lifetime. *Create* is a participial adjective; in a parallel instance Puck, blessing wedding beds, adds: 'And the issue there create / Ever shall be fortunate' (*A Midsummer Night's Dream*, 5.1.391–2). The *ate* ending survives in our own *elaborate*, also formed from the verb, or *incarnate*, though we don't now stress the final syllable. 'Created' doesn't rhyme or scan. Whose intervention might account for the change in Q2? The dramatist's? But to what end? The company's? Why do away with a perfectly good rhyming couplet, especially when there are many others in its immediate poetic vicinity (1.1.169–70; 179–80; 182–92)? Perhaps a scribe, or someone in the printing shop, then? Most editors used to choose Q1's 'create'; modern editorial preferences vary. Which reading would you pick?

A similar choice arises when Juliet protests to Romeo that she will be more faithful than others who might have held off longer (2.2.100–1). Here is Q1: 'But trust me gentleman I'll prove more true / Than they that have more cunning to be strange.' Q1 makes good sense to modern ears; it scans. Q2 gives the second line as: 'Than those that have coying to be strange.' Q2 doesn't scan but it's possible: *coying* could mean coyness. 'More cunning' has been the traditional preference, but some modern editors opt for 'coying', interpolating a supplementary 'more' or 'the' before the word to preserve the metre. Personally, I'm all for keeping things simple: in this instance Q1 works for me, but which would you choose?

Most editors prefer Romeo's 'agile' arm from Q1 to Q2's 'aged' one (3.1.168). A last instance before we consider the implications. Juliet tells the Friar she would go through any ordeal rather than agree to marry Paris. The horrors she lists include being shut in a charnel house, where bones that had emerged from old graves were stored, with, in Q2 'reeky shanks' (smelly leg bones) and 'yellow chapels skulls' (4.1.83). 'Chapels' might lie next to charnel houses, but it's difficult to see how the word makes much sense. Q1 offers a possible solution with its 'chaples'. *Chaps* or *chops* are jaws, cheeks; *chaples*, or *chapless*, describes skulls without the lower jaw.

Picking up a skull in the graveyard, Hamlet describes it as 'My Lady Worm's, chapless'; soon afterwards he mocks Yorick's skull: 'Quite chopfallen' (Folio *Hamlet*, 5.1.87–8; 190). The compound 'chapless' appears to have been Shakespeare's invention. Perhaps, then, a scribe or printer silently corrected an unfamiliar word. Most editors opt for Q1's 'chapless'.

Q2: The case for

At the level of detail, similar cases could easily be made in reverse. Shortly after Q2 suppresses Q1's rhyme on 'hate' and 'create' (1.1.174–5), it introduces (restores?) a rhyme between 'breast' and 'pressed' (184–5). Q2's 'Sad hours seem long' makes better sense than Q1's 'Sad hopes' (1.1.159); Q2's love that sees without eyes is more appropriately paradoxical that Q1's, which sees without 'laws' (1.1.170). Where at one moment Q1 nearly throws out the whole plot when it calls Juliet a Montague, Q2 puts the record straight (1.5.116). The Prologue in Q2 is a proper sonnet; the sonnet that precedes Act 2 exists only in Q2. More important, when the two texts are printed side by side, there are substantial gaps in Q1 at what we think of as the high points of the play, not least the exchange of vows in the orchard scene (2.2.120–35), the declaration of unspeakable love before the marriage (2.6.24–34), where Q1 offers only a brief exchange of banalities, and Juliet's anticipation of the wedding night, reduced in Q1 to a version of the first four lines (3.2.1–4). Q1 lacks much of Romeo's dying speech, including the recapitulation of the feast in the vault (5.3.85–6), the signs of life that Romeo so fatally misreads (92–6), and his rivalry with the figure of death (102–5), who finally engrosses him in their endless contract (115). Many of the Friar's reflections are missing from Q1.

While there are large areas of overlap, and some exact duplication between the two versions, and although both texts follow in outline the same story, Q2 differs in its alignment of the feuding families in the opening scene. Where Q2 shows the aggression rippling outwards from the servants to embrace the citizens and the old men before the Prince appears and parts them all, a stage direction in Q1 indicates that the citizens, Capulet and Montague enter with the Prince to separate the warring young men. The alignment of the older generation with law and order is a possibility, of course, but it gives us a much less divided Verona and offers, in consequence, less sense that the lovers are doomed from the outset by forces beyond their control.

In my view, we cannot do without Q2. Or, to put it differently, there is room for considerable doubt about whether, if by an accident of history only Q1 had survived, *Romeo and Juliet* would have secured the iconic status it now enjoys. No wonder Q2 seemed to so many editors to be the 'good' quarto.

Intermediaries

But how to account for its own gaps and errors? Q2 also presents problems, among them four lines ascribed to Romeo and then repeated by the Friar with a few very minor differences (2.2.188–91). A stage direction has Lady Capulet interrupting the parting of the lovers (3.5.36). A few lines later, Romeo takes over a speech ascribed to Juliet in Q1 – and then answers himself (54–9). In one notable instance, Mercutio's account of Queen Mab is printed in Q2 as prose and is more confusing in its depiction of the details of her diminutive coach. Where Q1 gives us a likely image (the spokes of the wheels are spiders' webs; the cover of the wagon is made of grasshoppers' wings; the sidestraps the team of little atomi use to pull the wagon are moonbeams, their collars the bones of crickets; the whip is gossamer), the picture in Q2 is harder to visualize: there it is the collars that are made of moonbeams, and the whip is the cricket bone; spiders feature twice, for their legs, as well as their webs (1.4.62–6). If Q1 was relegated as piratical, Q2 needed to be cleared of mistakes the author seemed unlikely to have made. Enter to this highly judgemental world of an earlier generation a new potential culprit, the compositor.

If, dear reader, this book you are reading contains errors, that is likely to be my fault or the editor's (ED. Please note. AU). Word processing reduces the gap between writing and print to almost nothing: I type my own words onto a screen; a printer is now a machine; you yourself are probably in a position to produce a page of immortal text and peel it off in an instant as perfect print. Things were very different in the early modern world. The playhouse would need more than one text but would not necessarily make the dramatist responsible for the duplicates – scribes and copyists might well do the work. The production of printed copy from a hand-written text was cumbrous and complicated, and involved further human intermediaries.

In the print shop the letters and punctuation marks existed in reverse, along with blank spaces, as small pieces of metal type, stored in the compartments of a large case. A compositor selected each character or space from its box, placing it upside-down in a small handheld tray, subsequently transferring the few lines assembled in this way to a table that would eventually hold enough type to fill one side of a large sheet. The type was then wedged into a frame, to be inked and pressed down on the paper. Evidently, there is room here for error, but the problem is compounded by the fact that one side of a whole sheet, or four pages of a quarto volume, was printed at a time. The subsequent folding process dictated that these pages were not consecutive. Before they began selecting type, compositors estimated how much of the material they could get into the spaces available. Often two worked at a time, one starting from the top of the first page, the other from the top of the next. The print shops were hot, noisy, inky and smelly (human urine played a part in the inking process); drafts of ale would replace lost sweat (no one drank the water). Only the professionalism of the compositors and their correctors stood between accuracy and chaos.

Given such circumstances, mistakes were a perpetual possibility. In one notable instance, the 1631 edition of the King James Bible included the commandment, 'Thou shalt commit adultery'. To assess the likelihood of printers' errors as the explanation of obscurities in Shakespeare's texts, good editors mastered the habits of early modern handwriting to see which words were easily misread; they took into account the location of the metal type in its boxes to gauge how one character might replace another by accident; they assessed the motives for squeezing the text to fit the spaces available, when an extra page could mean a whole extra sheet of expensive paper. This work became increasingly elaborate as anonymous compositors were distinguished from one another according to their habits of spelling and spacing, before judgements were made of their apparent levels of skill, expertise, dedication and reliability. The corresponding professionalism of editors, we might say, stands between us and changing literary tastes as the sole criterion of what Shakespeare might have written.

For an earlier generation, what was at stake, the object of desire, was a single, authoritative – which was to say authorial – version of the play, purged of the mistranscriptions introduced by actors, copyists and compositors. Shakespeare's manuscript, the one sure authority, fixed and indelible, must be made to shine through the veil of actual and potential error. As Brian Gibbons demonstrates in Arden 2, 'good' Q2 was thought to derive from Shakespeare's own hand; Q2, cleansed of mistakes, must therefore prevail, whatever the temptation to succumb to the blandishments of Q1. Fredson Bowers, one formidable protagonist in this struggle, was particularly exercised by the traditional preference for the 'bad' Q1's 'a rose / By any other name' over the 'good' Q2's 'any other word' (2.2.43–4). This was, he roundly declared in his book *On Editing Shakespeare* (1966), 'completely wrong', 'quite indefensible', a clear case of editors 'who do not know their business' coming between us and 'what Shakespeare actually wrote'. So serious was the error that the choice of 'name' over 'word' could be used 'as a touchstone to distinguish a textually untrained editor from a good one'. In future, such mistakes would be 'weeded out'. Unwilling to risk exposure as rank amateurs, a generation of editors quailed; discussion was suspended; 'a rose / By any other word' still stands as the prevailing choice.

Trouble

A large flock of editorial birds were pecking obediently at stories of memorial reconstruction, heaping praise and blame in equal measures on the 'good' quartos of the dramatist and the 'bad' quartos rehearsed by actors who betrayed him, while busily rescuing the 'good' texts from feckless compositors when, in the 1970s, some editors themselves began to wonder whether some of the differences between the consecutive printed texts might not more plausibly be explained by the assumption that they represented revisions. That hypothesis would replace the magisterial Shakespeare, who perceived the whole play immaculate in his head and transcribed it pure and entire onto the page, with a working dramatist, who composed much like other people, with false starts, flat passages, loose ends, afterthoughts and corrections, along with a more collective theatre, owned and operated by sharers, who wrote, performed and perhaps improved their outputs in the repertory as they went along.

Then in 1990 Paul Werstine, himself a distinguished editor, set the cat among pigeons with a vengeance. There was, he pointed out in the leading Shakespeare journal, no evidence for the tales of 'good' and 'bad' quartos – not a shred, nothing. No complete authorial manuscript of a Shakespeare play had ever been tracked down; no record traced an actor to any printing shop. Worse, the stories of memorial reconstruction had cemented themselves as truth even when their original proponents had put them forward as tentative hypotheses, or changed their minds later. In due course, this alternative view would gather speed. Speeches did not correspond between 'good' and 'bad' quartos consistently enough to single out any particular actors as the culprits. There is nothing to indicate that any play was ever stolen from Shakespeare's company; what is more, playbooks did not make the big money thought to motivate piracy. Laurie E. Maguire demonstrated in detail that virtually all the features thought to define 'bad' quartos could also be found in 'good' ones. Instead of clinging to old conjectures, it was time to acknowledge the possibility that changes were introduced in performance, by scribes who made fair copies, by compositors, as well as by the dramatist himself. The resulting play is altogether less definitive, less fixed than it once seemed, more dynamic, and in consequence more open to editorial choice.

Since then, a number of new hypotheses have emerged. Perhaps Q1 was an abridged version of the copy for Q2, which already existed more or less as we have it now – Q2 was, after all, too long to fit the 'two hours' traffic of our stage' promised by the Prologue (12). More radically, in *Shakespeare as Literary Dramatist* (2003) Lukas Erne put forward a case that we might have been wrong to see Shakespeare as indifferent to print and the posterity it allowed. If Q2 was too long for the conventional afternoon performance time, why would he write more than he needed to? Perhaps the 'good' quartos represented a version designed to be *read*, bought by people who wanted to think about the details, annotate and underline passages of their choice, or copy out maxims for their commonplace books. That would explain why Q2 of *Romeo and Juliet* is altogether more lyrical, poetic, reflective.

To my mind, all these conjectures have their problems. Cuts would not explain why Montague and Capulet side with the Prince in 1.1. The Folio version of the collected plays was assembled by actors but the version of *Romeo* they published derived ultimately from Q2, designed for 'reading', not the reduced stage version they must have had to hand. Or perhaps that was the point? The Folio was designed to memorialize a reading version for posterity, not to provide scripts for future acting companies? But that account would destroy the case often made for the special authority of the Folio, that it represents the nearest we have to the version early modern audiences actually saw. At the same time, speculative as they are, none of these hypotheses can be definitively ruled out. We are left in a degree of uncertainty about exactly who was responsible for what elements of the texts we have, and why.

Moreover, opinions vary about what exactly the modern editorial project is designed to produce. If the dramatist's manuscript is forever out of reach, are we aiming to recover a theatre production? But which? The earliest, with all its possible imperfections on its head, or a version improved as it made its way through the repertory?

What is to be done?

Does it matter? Can't we just leave the two main versions of *Romeo and Juliet* to a new and peaceful coexistence? In the case of other plays, where the gaps are even wider, editors have opted to do just that. In the Oxford and the Norton Shakespeares, two distinct versions of *King Lear* are printed consecutively; Arden 3 *Hamlet* now offers three different texts, while singling out Q2 as the most authoritative. Palgrave Macmillan evades the whole issue by presenting as Shakespeare's *Complete Works* a modernized version of the Folio edition of 1623.

Those solutions work well enough for scholars, who have the time, energy and access to assemble the options and make their own choices in the light of what evidence there is. But it leaves a problem for teachers, students, commentators and actors. What exactly is it that we are introducing to the young, or discussing, or performing? In those contexts Q1 alone would come across as little more than a curiosity, if a coherent one – *Romeo and Juliet* without the best bits. But Q2, unmodified by reference to Q1, stands to lose important meanings.

And besides, editors themselves have played a significant part in the construction of the play we have. Just how far would we want them to retreat from that responsibility? Printed in its original form, Q2 would present a very considerable puzzle to most modern readers.

In the first place, it is editors who supply the annotated list of roles that indicates in advance who everyone is. Speech prefixes alone would hardly work as a guide for first-time readers: in the original texts they are nothing if not inconsistent. Both versions play fast and loose with Juliet's parents: Capulet is occasionally 'Fa[ther]' or 'Old Man'; Lady Capulet is variously 'Wife', 'La[dy]', 'Old La', 'Capu Wife', 'Moth[er]' and 'Mo'. Sometimes these characters slip from one to another and back in consecutive speeches. In addition, the early modern texts have no act and scene divisions: the play unfolds continuously without breaks to indicate changes of time and place. The Folio *Romeo and Juliet*, which unaccountably omits the Prologue, opens grandly, with '*Actus Primus. Scœna Prima*' – and then sinks back exhausted, to print the rest of the play undivided. Editors traditionally tidy all this up for ease of access.

Second, one of my favourite passages is in practice the work of an editor:

> What's Montague? It is nor hand nor foot
> Nor arm nor face nor any other part
> Belonging to a man. O be some other name. (2.2.40–2)

To this neat combination of what most concerns Juliet in love (the name and the parts of the body belonging to a man, including any others not specified), Q1 contributes: 'What's Montague? It is nor hand nor foot / Nor arm, nor face, nor any other part.' This seems to promise something it fails to deliver. Q2, meanwhile, offers, 'What's Montague? It is nor hand nor foot, / Nor arm nor face, O be some other name / Belonging to a man'. Here 'belonging to a man' is a property of the name, not the parts of the body, which seems to miss a possible point. Had a compositor misread the instructions? It was the eighteenth-century editor Edmond Malone who, by incorporating all the phrases from both texts and reversing the last two from Q2, produced the solution that has become familiar to us by pleasing most subsequent editors.

If (and I freely concede the *if*) Malone's intervention is legitimate, then what isn't? It was not until the twentieth century that editors ventured to introduce a word that often restores the attention of a flagging classroom, when Mercutio exclaims, 'O Romeo, that she were, O that she were / An open-arse and thou a poperin pear!' (2.1.37–8). Q1 coyly ventures 'An open *Et cætera*', while Q2 settles for 'An open, or thou a Poperin Pear', which, metrically speaking, leaves a syllable missing. Editors unearthed the dialect name for the medlar and all was light.

I personally would not want to undo any of this work, but the consequence must be a slightly freer idea of what constitutes a text. We must give up on the reconstruction of the authorial manuscript, pure and undiminished from the mind of the dramatist, as an ideal that cannot be realized. What sort of ideal was it, after all, that excluded from the process of composition Shakespeare's theatrical colleagues, who would contribute to making the play work on the stage? We had better acknowledge the intervention of copyists and compositors. We should, in other words, settle for what we have as the basis of the best we can hope for: a play that can be read, taught, performed, but always with the proviso that it is a conflation, a composite, an unstable assembly of editorial choices, based on varying degrees of skill, knowledge and judgement, and open to perpetual question.

The clown

Is the loss of confidence in the pristine authorial text an unmitigated disaster? I think not. Once we acknowledge the instability of the play we have, no longer insisting on the definitive mono-text, we allow ourselves scope for considering the various loose ends rigorously excised from the single version that aspired to authority on the basis of its coherence. Among these, I find myself fascinated by the figure of a clown, who weaves his tenuous way uncertainly through the two early versions to indicate that Elizabethan audiences might (just *might*) have seen a rather different kind of play from the one we have come to know.

Here is his story. In Q2, as Capulet and Paris begin the discussion that will end in an invitation to the feast (1.2), the opening stage direction reads 'Enter Capulet, County Paris, and the Clown'. This last proves to be the illiterate figure who will in due course be instructed to invite the people on the written list, but by that time he will have been redesignated 'Servant', or 'Servingman', as he is in Q1. His role, however, is clowning. The comedy of his exchanges with 'the learned' (1.2.43) depends on his baffled readiness to give up the struggle when Romeo teases him and his apparent inability to supply a straight answer to a simple question.

We next glimpse the clown in Q1, abruptly summoning Lady Capulet to organize the feast (1.3.101–4). Here again, the urgency of the moment produces potential for laughter. In the Q1 version: '*Clown*. Madam you are called for, supper is ready, the Nurse cursed in the pantry, all things in extremity, make haste for I must be gone to wait.' Clowning can be as much physical as verbal (think Mr Bean): a good comic could wonderfully communicate his impatience with the discussion upstairs, his anxiety about his own obligations, and the chaos in the kitchen that contrasts so palpably with the serious exchanges that have been taking place concerning Juliet's suitor. In Q2 'Clown' has become 'Serving[man]'.

But it is Q2 that betrays the identity of this shadowy clown. In 4.5, when Juliet's bed-curtains have been closed, and the musicians who have come to play her to her wedding begin to pack away their instruments, the stage direction reads: '*Enter Will Kemp*' (99). Will Kemp was not a fictional figure but a sharer in the Shakespeare company and its resident clown from 1595–9. In the speech prefixes he promptly becomes Peter ('Servingman' in Q1) but not before the name of the performer suggests the possibility that the not-very-funny exchanges that follow might once have been hilarious. Kemp was legendary, a physical comedian, renowned for his jigs. When he left the company, he danced from London to Norwich in nine days and then wrote about it. He is thought to have exploited a squint and a rustic accent. He was also notably independent. When Hamlet instructs the players on the kind of performance he wants from them in the all-important *Mousetrap* designed to make Claudius betray his guilt, he adds: 'And let those that play your clowns speak no more than is set down for them.' There are, he goes on, those who will laugh themselves, and set on the audience, without reference to the play before them. 'That's villainous and shows a most pitiful ambition in the fool that uses it' (*Hamlet*, 3.2.39–46). Was Will Kemp among those who extemporized to comic effect?

Either way, Kemp evidently played Peter, who has only a handful of lines, some of them commonly cut in modern performances, where their point is no longer intelligible. But in the scene where Peter appears as the Nurse's man, his one speech can bring the house down. I know this from experience. At my single-sex school, stage-struck but with no acting talent whatever, I was allowed to play Peter. I was to make nothing of the exchanges between the Nurse and the young men; I was to stare vacantly into the distance, munching a doughnut; on these terms, I could not do much harm. My speech, despite my best efforts to make it theatrical, came out as a monotone: 'I saw no man use you at his pleasure. If I had, my weapon should quickly have been out' (2.4.151–2). I was consequently astonished by the gale of laughter that greeted this intervention. The audience, way ahead of me, had grasped the innuendo, as well as the absurdity of this stolid figure declaring a readiness to fight – or to join in the sexual harassment.

Peter is the Nurse's man. But Will makes another fleeting appearance in Q1 that suggests the possibility of a more pervasive role. As Capulet bustles to prepare the wedding feast, a servant comes on with logs for the fire. They are not dry enough, Capulet complains: 'Choose drier. Will will tell thee where thou shalt fetch them.' The servant replies that he has a head to fetch logs without advice, which leads to a joke about how he is a 'loggerhead' (blockhead). In Q2 'Will' has become 'Peter' (4.4.16). The servant can manage on his own, he protests, 'and never trouble Peter for the matter' (18). This suggests, first, that Will/Peter has already established enough of a presence with the audience to be memorable in his absence and, second, that his place in the household is not confined to accompanying the Nurse. He is, instead, a source of some domestic authority.

Putting all this together, I conjecture (and it is no more than that) that Will Kemp/Peter is the illiterate servant in 1.2 and the figure who summons Lady Capulet in 1.3, as well as the Nurse's man and the tormentor of the musicians. But why stop there? If we are in the realm of speculation (and we are), it is worth remembering that this figure's third alternative designation throughout is 'Servingman'. What if Will Kemp/Peter is the servant who calls for Potpan as they prepare the first feast, looking forward with relish to his piece of marzipan and the arrival of Susan Grindstone and Nell (1.5.1–15), not to mention the one who appears for the sake of making a now largely impenetrable joke about good cooks licking their fingers (4.2.1–8)?

The inclusion of a clown of Kemp's stature would explain these repeated but otherwise incidental downstairs allusions. It would also shift the balance of the play towards comedy, though without allowing the clown to confront high tragedy directly. He features in the Capulet household, perhaps helping to define it as absurd, but he does not encounter the lovers themselves.

Or does he? One puzzle remains. As Romeo approaches the tomb with the spade and crowbar, the Q2 stage direction reads, '*Enter Romeo and Peter*'. In Q1 the hero is accompanied by Balthasar, his man, just as we should expect. But Q2's subsequent speech prefixes all call him 'Peter', and 'Peter' he remains in Q3 and the Folio, where it is Peter who calls the Watch. On the other hand, when it comes to the final explanations, the figure who claims to have been there with Romeo in Q1 and Q2 is named Balthasar and in F 'Boy' (5.3.272–7). Paris's page calls the Watch.

It is hard to believe that a Capulet servant could also serve Romeo. Moreover, Balthasar's role is not remotely comic. 'Peter' makes no sense in this context, unless Kemp doubled as a straight man. However, Romeo's servant is called Peter in the main source, Arthur Brooke's *Romeus and Juliet* (2697). Perhaps the name is just a vestige – and a warning against an eagerness to tie up loose ends too closely?

The Nurse

Nonetheless, one other loose end tempts speculation yet again. This time the evidence is far less substantial and it might well be that I'd be wise to heed the previous warning. Even so ...

Finding Juliet as she thinks dead, the Nurse, beside herself with grief, calls in both Q1 and Q2 for aqua vitae (brandy, 4.5.16). Although the purpose is not specified, the assumption is that the spirits are designed to revive her charge. However, this is not the first time brandy has featured in the play. In Q1, when she returns from meeting Romeo, teasing Juliet as she withholds his message, the Nurse complains: 'Lord how my bones ache. Oh where's my man? Give me some aqua vitae.' Partisans of Q2 ignore this, on the grounds that it seems to have been transposed from 3.2, where the Nurse once again returns to Juliet, this time with the news of Tybalt's death. 'Ah, where's my man? Give me some aqua vitae. / These griefs, these woes, these sorrows make me old' (88–9). But suppose we kept both? And suppose the brandy in 4.5 is only ostensibly for Juliet?

Angry with his daughter, and infuriated by the Nurse's irrepressible interventions, Capulet enjoins her to 'smatter with your gossips'. When this fails to silence her, he tries again: 'Utter your gravity o'er a gossip's bowl' (3.5.171, 174). A gossip's bowl contained ale that would no doubt fuel the rumour mill. In Capulet's enraged eyes she belongs with her tattling cronies and their tipple. I confess that I would make little of this, were it not for another loose end, this time in the main source of the play. There, you remember, Arthur Brooke's moralizing preface bore so little relation to the story he tells that there seemed no connection between his sympathetic narrative and the prefatory reference to the dangerous influence of 'drunken gossips'. The only possible candidate for this doubtful honour was the Nurse (see Chapter 4), but the words remained a puzzle. Did that very conundrum sow a seed in the mind of the dramatist? Did it weave itself, half-formed, into the beginnings of a pattern in *Romeo and Juliet*? Was the Nurse conceived, however momentarily, however half-heartedly, as given to drink? And did a surviving theatrical tradition lead Thomas Otway, when he adapted the play in 1679, to have his Nurse explain her skittishness with the hero by telling him she has been drinking aqua vitae, becoming agitated later about recovering a mysterious cordial-bottle?

But adaptations are another story.

Writing matters

It's time to turn your own hand to making some of the choices editors confront in their efforts to generate a single text from the material available. The best way to see at a glance the differences between the two quarto texts is to study them in parallel on facing pages.

Q1 (1597)

Enter Prince with others.

Prin: What early mischief calls us up so soon.
Capt: O noble Prince, see here
Where *Juliet* that hath lien entombed two days,
Warm and fresh bleeding, *Romeo* and County *Paris*
Likewise newly slain.
Prin: Search seek about to find the murderers.

Enter old Capulet and his Wife.

Capu: What rumour's this that is so early up?
Moth: The people in the streets cry *Romeo*,
And some on *Juliet*: as if they alone
Had been the cause of such a mutiny.

Capu. See Wife, this dagger hath mistook:
For (lo) the back is empty of young Montague,
And it is sheathed in our daughter's breast.

Enter old Montague.

Prin: Come *Montague*, for thou art early up,
To see thy son and heir more early down.
Mont: Dread Sovereign, my wife is dead tonight,
And young *Benvolio* is deceased too:
What further mischief can there yet be found?
Prin: First come and see, then speak.
Mont: O thou untaught, what manners is in this
To press before thy father to a grave.
Prin: Come seal your mouths of outrage for a while,
And let us seek to find the Authors out
Of such a heinous and seld seen mischance.

Bring forth the parties in suspicion.

Q2 (1599)

Enter the Prince.

Prin. What misadventure is so early up,
That calls our person from our morning rest?

Enter Capels.

Ca. What should it be that is so shrike abroad? [shrieked]
Wife. O the people in the street cry *Romeo*,
Some *Juliet*, and some *Paris*, and all run
With open outcry toward our Monument.
Pr. What fear is this which startles in your ears?
Watch. Sovereign, here lies the County *Paris* slain,
And *Romeo* dead, and *Juliet* before,
Warm and new killed.
Prin. Search, seek and know how this foul murder comes.
Watch. Here is a Friar, and Slaughter *Romeos* man,
With instruments upon them, fit to open
These dead men's tombs.

Enter Capulet and his wife.

Ca. O heavens! O wife look how our daughter bleeds!
This dagger hath mista'en, for lo his house
Is empty on the back of Montague,
And it mis-sheathed in my daughters bosom.
Wife. O me, this sight of death, is as a Bell
That warns my old age to a sepulchre.

Enter Montague.

Prin. Come *Montague*, for thou art early up
To see thy son and heir, now earling down.
Mon. Alas my liege, my wife is dead tonight,
Grief of my son's exile hath stopped her breath.
What further woe conspires against mine age?
Prin. Look and thou shalt see.
Mon. O thou untaught, what manners is in this,
To press before thy father to a grave?
Prin. Seal up the mouth of outrage for a while,
Till we can clear these ambiguities,
And know their spring, their head, their true descent,
And then will I be general of your woes,
And lead you even to death, meantime forbear,
And let mischance be slave to patience,
Bring forth the parties of suspicion.

In the absence of expertise in Elizabethan handwriting and printing, the value of the exercise may lie as much in the consideration of the implications of your choices as in the solutions themselves. I have selected a passage where at first the alternatives seem less than momentous (5.3.188–222): in that respect it is more characteristic than some of the more controversial instances I have discussed. But closer analysis shows that there are decisions to be made, not only at the level of individual wording but also about where the emphasis lies. How can we resolve some of the puzzles? What difference does it make if the Capulets, rather than the Watch, have first access to the Prince? How does the role of representatives of law and order vary between the two versions? Would Benvolio's death affect the ending?

On the evidence of this passage, are you more inclined to favour the view that Q2 revises Q1, that Q1 abridges Q2, or that Q1 belongs on the stage while Q2 is a reading version? Or would you rather keep your options open? And finally, what do you think is the project that should be kept in mind when producing a composite text? What are we trying to uncover? Shakespeare's intentions? An early modern performance? A lasting memorial for readers? A workable modern text for actors, or for the classroom? And, whatever your answers to these questions, what price do we pay for choosing between the different possibilities?

CHAPTER SIX

Afterlives: Language through time

Adaptability

Romeo and Juliet has been large and generous. In the four centuries since the first performance, the play has made space for a wide variety of interpretations and revisions. It has been put to work in support of a range of causes, rewritten to suit new notions of decorum, reimagined in popular and successful films, as well as reconstituted in the form of opera, ballet, more than one orchestral work and at least one musical. When tastes change, as meanings vary and values alter, what people turn out to want from the play shifts too. Different issues come to the fore, new questions arise, and *Romeo and Juliet* remains ready to deliver. Modifications push and pull at its shape, while enough of its language, plot, or structure survives in the reinscriptions for us to recognize a debt to Shakespeare's tragedy.

All interpretations are the effect of choices – of emphasis, focus, priority. The play changes in the 1660s, when it moves from the early modern open-air playing place to the indoor stage, framed by a proscenium arch, as this new kind of theatre fosters altered assumptions about what a play ought to be. If some productions reinterpret the tragedy more radically than others, all performances since Shakespeare's time are to a degree adaptations: we can't now recover the exact sights and sounds, meanings and values familiar to those earlier audiences, and when we try, in all-male productions or the 2004 version in old pronunciation, what Shakespeare's playgoers took for granted as natural becomes for us a historical curiosity. Meanwhile, a switch from stage to screen changes more than the mode of representation: the theatre, however small, preserves a degree of distance and legitimates the heroic character of verse drama; photography, by contrast, generates expectations of realism, while close-up and montage may direct our gaze in a way that theatre does not. In this more intimate context the heroic may seem out of place.

An adapted text is not the original, and not best assessed in terms of its fidelity to the original, but in its difference. It can reveal much about the culture that produces it. But if it is an adaptation at all, it also captures some feature of its source, even if not the one we might most expect. When Baz Luhrmann claims to remake *Romeo and Juliet* in the way Shakespeare might have presented it *if he had been a filmmaker*, he is defining a transposition that changes the play. Does he, in the process, also draw attention to aspects of work that we might not otherwise foreground?

In the light of their own and their culture's preoccupations, directors abridge, amplify or realign. How far do cuts alter not just the balance but the meaning of the play? Does it change the emphasis significantly when Franco Zeffirelli's film of 1968 takes out the Apothecary and inserts Friar John's experience in the plague-ridden house? How does it affect our experience of the tragedy if the actor playing Juliet is 15 – or 50? What difference does it make if an interpretation ignores Mercutio's scepticism, or invests him with his own desiring interiority?

Modernization

A performance taking the second quarto of 1599 as its text lasts more than three hours – longer, in other words, than 'the two hours' traffic of our stage' indicated by the Prologue (12). A play where the language is 400 years old cannot necessarily be relied on to sustain the attention of a modern audience for so long. Might a director be wise to reduce the material with a view to fulfilling the Prologue's promise? In his book about 'rescripting' Shakespeare on the modern stage, Alan Dessen quotes one director's advice on the issue: 'shorten each scene as much as possible ... eliminate everything that might confuse an audience ... cut all characters who are unnecessary to the scene ... cut all scenes which do not advance the story ... cut or change all words that are archaic or obscure.'

On this basis, the musicians generally go (4.5.96–141), along with a number of the downstairs exchanges. The recapitulation of the story in the final scene is often deleted, as well as parts of the Friar's reflection on herbs and their properties. Some words are updated to promote understanding. In his 2009 production at Shakespeare's Globe in London, Dominic Dromgoole replaced 'runagate' with 'renegade' (3.5.89); Baz Luhrmann in *William Shakespeare's Romeo + Juliet* (1996) gives 'confession' in place of the recurring 'shrift' and sometimes prefers 'priest' or 'Father' to 'friar'. Where in Q2 Mercutio invites Tybalt to draw his sword 'out of his pilcher by the ears' (3.1.79–80) Dromgoole borrowed from Q1 to create the more intelligible 'pluck your rapier out of his scabbard'. From the same source, he introduced a modern-sounding phrase into 4.2, where Juliet's parents debate the day of her marriage to Paris: 'I say tomorrow', insisted Dromgoole's Capulet, 'while she's in the mood.'

It would be a purist indeed who would object to these minor verbal modifications. But arguably cuts, however slight they might seem, change the experience of the audience. In *Rescripting Shakespeare* Alan Dessen also quotes a manual published in 1983, which takes a very different line from the first director he quotes: 'If you trust the play enough to stage it, trust its author', and 'If you alter or cut whenever you have difficulty you may miss something important'.

The manual surely has a point: change the words and you change the meaning. In this respect, too, Dromgoole's 2009 Globe version drew on Q1 for the benefit of modern playgoers. (I should say at once that this was in general a magnificent production, now available on DVD, and the one I would most strongly recommend for anyone who wants to see the play staged. My doubts over details are offered as talking points, not judgements.) At the moment when Capulet takes Montague's hand, Q2 gives: 'This is my daughter's jointure, for no more / Can I demand' (5.3.297–8); Dromgoole's Capulet said: 'There is my daughter's dowry, for now no more / Can I bestow on her. That's all I have.' Dowries are still intelligible, jointures less so, but this interpolation from Q1 makes a difference to the way we understand the exchange. In Q2 Juliet's father is saying that Montague's hand is all he is asking as the bridegroom's settlement on the couple: the only 'jointure' is to be a joining of hands. Q1's 'dowry' reverses the position: dowries are provided by the bride's family and Capulet is extending his hand instead because that's all he can now give her – in the circumstances, a financial settlement is irrelevant. Or does 'That's all I have' mean he can't afford any more? Suddenly we are led off into the speculation that the Capulets are hard up; was that why the marriage to Paris was so urgent? But if it's true, how can Capulet promise to reciprocate with a golden statue of Romeo? Although I have argued for taking Q1 seriously, in this instance I can't help thinking that these thoughts are likely to distract playgoers from the moving moment of reconciliation that brings the tragedy to a form of resolution.

Now let's take a more difficult case: the consequences of eradicating a whole speech. What might be missed by the common practice of deleting the Friar's recapitulation of the story in the final scene (5.3.231–64)? After all, we know what happened; we have been witnesses to it all along; we hardly need to hear the story all over again. But there is a difference: the Friar is now revealing the facts to an on-stage audience who cannot be counted on to sympathize. The Prince, the Watch, and the parents of the protagonists will all judge his part in the story. For a moment, in consequence, we are invited to perceive the romance from a new perspective: the marriage of the lovers was 'stol'n'; Juliet 'with wild looks' prevailed on her mentor to supply the potion when she threatened suicide; in the tomb she rejected his counselled patience and instead, 'too desperate', 'did violence on herself'. We may conclude that this account is partial, the Friar's attempt to exonerate himself, but something of the desperation, the recklessness stays in the memory to complicate the idealizing final image, naturalized by Victorian painting, as well as by Zeffirelli and Luhrmann, of the lovers as victims of a violence that comes only from outside them, as they lie clasped in a tender and strangely bloodless death.

The concept

Sometimes the modifications are more purposeful, designed to accord with the director's concept of the work, or with the constraints of a specific situation. When George Cukor filmed the play in 1936, the actor playing Juliet was 36 years old and Romeo ten years older. All references to Juliet's age were deleted.

Modern interpretations are inclined to develop individual relationships and characters out of hints in the text. This adds local interest and gives the actors a backstory they can play to. Sometimes Juliet's parents are at war with each other: Zeffirelli's film makes much of this conflict from the moment it inventively turns Capulet's observation on the perils of early marriage into a direct comment on his own (1.2.13). Marital hostility, seen as distressing in the film, was to become a source of comedy at the Globe in Dromgoole's production. Dromgoole also made Paris something of a joke, while Baz Luhrmann's Paris embodies dull, clean-cut orthodoxy as *Time*'s 'Bachelor of the Year'. The effect in each case is to simplify Juliet's choice: there can be, after all, no contest between such a Paris and the romantic Romeo. In the process, the parents are seen to be hopelessly out of touch with true love: how could they imagine such a husband for their daughter? The gap between these generations evidently cannot be bridged.

But it is Mercutio who most consistently attracts detailed psychologizing characterization. One of the sources of Shakespeare's infinite adaptability is surely that, while his characters are given such distinctive voices, they are what (and how) they speak. That is to say, they speak from a clearly defined position, typifying a range of familiar ways of being: Romeo is a lover; the Nurse is garrulous and pragmatic; Capulet is a well-meaning but irascible father, and so on. It is because they are representative in this way that they elicit such recognition across the centuries. Mercutio is the friend who fears the lads are losing Romeo to love.

This relationship is wonderfully reinscribed in the musical *West Side Story* (dir. Robert Wise and Jerome Robbins, 1961), which rereads the feud as a turf war between conflicting New York gangs, the Sharks Puerto Rican, the Jets second-generation immigrants who lay claim to the territory against the newcomers. Tony, the movie's Romeo, has grown out of the Jets, where Baby John still reads Marvel comics: Tony has a job; he is in love. Only Maria's pressure on him to stop the violence induces him to attend the rumble that will fatally revive his allegiance to his old friend Riff, leader of the Jets.

In other instances, however, after two centuries of the novel and the advent of psychoanalysis, not to mention soap opera, there is an impulse to look behind what is said for its occluded meanings, the hidden agendas and unconscious imperatives that seem to *us* to motivate human behaviour. It is very common in modern productions to see Mercutio's exuberant flight of fancy in the Queen Mab speech tail off into an apparently unaccountable melancholy. 'Peace, peace, Mercutio, peace, / Thou talk'st of nothing', Romeo insists. 'True', Mercutio sadly concedes, 'I talk of dreams ...' (1.4.95–6).

Why is he sorrowful? What are these dreams? Are they of Romeo as an object of desire? It's possible, of course. And this interpretation is a welcome intervention in the current process of naturalizing a variety of sexual identities; for that alone it is to be endorsed on stage and screen. Who in their right mind would want to be without Baz Luhrmann's magnificent cross-dressed Mercutio in silver wig and bra, white miniskirt and stockings, on the staircase at the Capulet fancy-dress party, as he commands all eyes with his performance of 'Young Hearts Run Free'? This Mercutio is sparkling, seductive, glorious.

And yet the representation of a desiring Mercutio excludes the scepticism towards love that I discussed in Chapter 2, psychologizing it as personal resentment against a rival lover. Modern productions offer a range of sexualities at the price of a range of attitudes to love. Has scepticism about love become unintelligible? Perhaps we are all romantics now, unable to recognize reservations about passion. Perhaps, in other words, our secular culture has come to rate true love so highly, to invest it with such magical redemptive powers, that doubts about the extravagance of desire seem themselves perverse, in need of psychological explanation.

Anachronism?

There will be more to say about Mercutio's sexuality in Chapter 7. For the moment I am suggesting that a Mercutio who is in love may be anachronistic. But isn't all adaptation anachronistic? That, surely, is the point. Performance to varying degrees adjusts an old play to the tastes and concerns of a modern audience. In the case of *Romeo and Juliet* the process of adjustment began early. When David Garrick rewrote the play to be enacted in eighteenth-century dress in 1748 and again in 1750, his declared purpose was to 'clear the original as much as possible from the jingle and quibble which were always thought a great objection to performing it'. By the standards of the time, it was not only the puns that were unacceptable but also the rhyming couplets. Out with them! In the second version, Rosaline was also banished, on the grounds that 'the sudden change of Romeo's love from Rosaline to Juliet was a blemish in his character'. In other words, there could be only one Ms Right. Who would have thought that Victorian values had set in nearly a century before that queen ascended the throne? But romantic love had by now exiled arranged marriages for good, and true love had better be constant. As it happened, it would be variants of Garrick's version of the play that held the stage for nearly a century, well into the reign of Victoria herself.

Juliet was now Romeo's object of desire from the start. The excision of Rosaline had the unfortunate side effect that the 'straight leg, and quivering thigh / And the demesns that there adjacent lie' in Garrick's 2.1 now belonged to Juliet. But Rosaline hadn't quite disappeared: she was to return for an instant, probably by mistake, as Romeo's tormentor in 2.4. If Romeo was now unblemished by a previous love, Garrick cleaned up the play in other ways, too. His Juliet was not yet eighteen (and the Nurse had eight teeth, cf. 1.3.13–15); this saved Romeo from the imputation of child-abduction. Death's shocking possession of Juliet is duly reduced to sexual (and metrical) propriety. Shakespeare gives: 'the night before thy wedding day / Hath death lain with thy wife. There she lies, / Flower as she was, deflowered by him' (4.5.35–7); Garrick renders this: 'the night before the wedding day / Death has embraced thy wife: see, there she lies. / Flower as she was, nipped in the bud by him!'

The eighteenth century perceived Shakespeare as a wild, untutored genius in need of cultivation. On the one hand, he was hugely admired; on the other, he belonged to a more barbaric age and his education had been sadly lacking.

Decorum now necessitated a more classical drama, uniformly elevated morally and linguistically. Garrick's brief preface to his *Romeo and Juliet* tells the whole contradictory story: the greatest actor-manager of his time has revised the play 'with as little injury to the original as possible'. On the one hand, the original should not be injured; on the other, the original needs radical revision. But Garrick was not the first to rewrite the play. Theophilus Cibber had also produced a version in 1744, preparing some of the ground in advance. Already much of the comedy has disappeared and Cibber puts Juliet's behaviour in a dubious perspective when Lady Capulet, surprised at her initial resistance to an arranged marriage, asks: 'What sensual, lewd companion of the night / Have you been holding conversation with, / From open window, at a midnight hour?' (1.3).

These classicizing revisers preferred to protect playgoers from the diction that we find most Shakespearean, the oscillation between the heroic and the everyday. Cibber deletes the Nurse's story of Juliet's weaning from her dug (1.3.27–33); Garrick keeps the tale but calls the body part a breast. Heroic themes require consistently poetic vocabulary and Cibber accordingly rewrites the opening of Juliet's wedding-night speech (3.2.1–2): the sun god ought to have a 'mansion', not a mere 'lodging'; Phaeton is no longer a 'wagoner' but a 'charioteer'. (Garrick also opts for the mansion but concedes the wagoner.) Anachronism here presents itself as improvement.

In our own postmodern times, however, anachronism has become a cause for celebration. In *Shakespeare in Love* (dir. John Madden, 1998) Will, who in sixteenth-century dress is shortly to begin writing *Romeo and Juliet*, has on his desk a mug labelled 'A Present from Stratford upon Avon' with a picture of Anne Hathaway's cottage. The screenplay repeatedly invites our delighted laughter by swerving between Shakespearean diction and modern colloquialism. But it is Baz Luhrmann who is the master of witty anachronism. In *William Shakespeare's Romeo + Juliet* he manages to retain the references to swords and rapiers in the text by turning them into the brand names of guns. In a modern (or futuristic) Verona Beach the 'Globe Theatre' is now a pool hall; Sycamore Grove, where Romeo walks alone (1.1.119), has become a ruined cinema; a poster advertises Prospero Scotch Whiskey [sic] with the slogan 'Such stuff as dreams are made on' (*The Tempest*, 4.1.156–7). If anachronism is inevitable, best to make the most of it – with a wink at knowing viewers.

Good chronological narratives of the afterlives of *Romeo and Juliet* are available and in what remains of this chapter I shall confine myself to picking out certain issues that have concerned us in the course of this book: first gender, then violence, and finally genre.

Decline

In Chapter 2 I proposed that the play established a remarkable degree of parity between its lovers: this passion is mutual, symmetrical, equal. Remarkably, it is Juliet who describes their wedding night in a speech that is both lyrical and sexually aware. The love scenes credit her with as many overtures as Romeo, perhaps more, while Romeo is to a degree feminized by love. As if to confirm an element of interchangeability between the protagonists, the play's final couplet reverses the order of their names as these appear in the title of the play: 'For never was a story of more woe / Than this of Juliet and her Romeo' (5.3.309–10). Neither, we may understand, has primacy here; the story, like the love scenes, like the enjoyment of the wedding night, belongs to them both equally.

But the history of the relations between men and women indicates that Shakespeare's utopian vision was too good to last. In 1600 women were just as capable as men of enjoying sex; by 1800 men were driven by the desire for sexual conquest, while women were there to restrain them. The descent from the Shakespearean ideal set in early. Although we know that Pepys saw it in 1662 and didn't like it, we mainly lose track of *Romeo and Juliet* in the seventeenth century until it reappears as a component of Thomas Otway's play *Caius Marius* in 1679, where the tragedy is incorporated into a story from Roman history. Otway hands passages of Shakespeare's dialogue between the lovers to Young Marius and Lavinia, with modifications to fit the reduced space, as well as to accommodate changing tastes. Rosaline is excised, and Lavinia revives before Marius dies, allowing for devoted exchanges between them. Although from the beginning Lavinia displays a resolute resistance to arranged marriage – 'lawful rape', as she terms it (2.1) – Otway deletes Juliet's other minor acts of defiance in fending off first her mother with a series of double entendres (3.5.81–102), and then Paris with polite indifference (4.1.18–38).

Lavinia is not allowed to talk about sex. The exchange about 'satisfaction' (2.2.125–6) is modified to erase the innuendo: 'Why wilt thou leave me so unsatisfied?' asks Marius. 'What wouldst thou have?' counters Lavinia innocently (2.2). Deep cuts are imposed on the wedding-night speech (3.2.1–31): Juliet's anticipation of their amorous rites, the stainless maidenhoods that will be lost and won, as well as strange love grown confident with practice, are all removed and, in case this appears no more than a device to save time, a further revealing excision excludes the reference to Juliet sold but yet to be enjoyed. 'Oh! I have bought the mansion of a love, / But not possessed it …', exclaims Lavinia, leaving the thought uncompleted (3.2).

Moreover, Otway's heroine will in due course turn out to be properly feminine, according to the now prevailing meaning of the term. Finding Marius Senior starving in the wilderness outside Rome, she supplies him with food and water, thus reconciling the patriarch to his son's marriage to the daughter of his enemy. Such a woman would evidently have made a good wife and mother. Young Marius duly changes too; there is no more talk of effeminacy. Instead, he puts off his wedding night with Lavinia until he has won approval in the wars. The doubts about the merits of violence that characterize *Romeo and Juliet* have disappeared from Otway's play: now it is the readiness to fight that defines a hero. While Lavinia is sexually reticent, as well as nurturing and caring, Marius has become a real man. Out of Shakespeare's parity between the lovers Otway has drawn opposite sexes.

Many of his changes were preserved when Romeo and Juliet returned to the stage under their own names in the 1740s. Cibber wakes Juliet before Romeo's death, as does Garrick. Cibber also keeps the reference to arranged marriage as 'lawful rape' (1.3) and retains the substance of Juliet's small-scale defiance of her mother and Paris. But, like Otway, he cuts the sex out of her wedding-night speech. Although his Romeo is no Marius, at one moment he displays a heroic disregard of death. When it comes to the Prince's sentence, Cibber's Romeo affirms: 'He can but doom me dead, and I'm prepared' (3.3). Shakespeare's reversal of the title names in the final couplet evidently did not suit the new times: in Cibber's version, 'Never true lovers' story did impart / More real anguish to a humane heart'. I leave it to you to decide whether this is an improvement.

Garrick, too, rewrote the final couplet: 'From private feuds, what dire misfortunes flow; / Whate'er the cause, the sure effect is WOE.' If in his adaptation of the play there is slightly more of Shakespeare, no indication remains that Juliet knows anything about sex and, at the reference to sale and enjoyment, Garrick reproduces Otway's elision. All in all, by the time Thomas and Henrietta Bowdler issued their cleaned-up *Family Shakespeare* early in the nineteenth century, their work on this play had mostly been done for them, although to be on the safe side they removed all reference to the mansion of a love, bought and sold, possessed or to be enjoyed.

Juliet's newfound purity and passivity persisted on the stage. Henry Irving, who produced a version of the play in 1882, based his text on Shakespeare but cut it severely to make way for spectacular scenery. He, too, deleted Juliet's mild resistance to her mother and most of her management of Paris; his version of the wedding night followed Garrick's cuts.

It seems that for more than two centuries after Shakespeare's own period, the proprieties accustomed playgoers to a naive and much less independent Juliet.

When it came to Romeo, however, the eighteenth-century adapters allowed talk of his effeminacy to survive. Garrick, who played the part for many years, evidently relished the histrionic opportunities offered by the hero's suffering in the scene with the Friar (3.3). But there would be a price to pay for this indulgence. While Garrick's version continued to be performed for another hundred years or so, after his death tastes were to change again. As the British upper lip stiffened in the nineteenth century, the role of Romeo grew less attractive to male actors, who were repelled by the extravagance of his feelings. Victorian boys didn't cry.

Rescue?

Remarkably enough, it was a woman who rescued Romeo, when the American Charlotte Cushman thrilled London in the part, using Shakespeare's text for the first time since the seventeenth century. Instead of evading Romeo's emotion, Cushman gave it full vent, to the delight of the commentators. The scene that had proved most embarrassing for male actors was now singled out for praise; in the words of *The Times* reviewer on 30 December 1845,

> The grief in Friar Lawrence's cell, when Romeo set forth the sorrows of his banishment in tones of an ever-increasing anguish, till at last it reached its culminating point, and he dashed himself on the ground with real despair, took the house by storm.

Evidently such fervour was acceptable in a Romeo played by a woman. It seems that an element of gender ambiguity could save both Shakespeare's play and Victorian masculinity.

Indeed, another reviewer noted that 'It is open to question whether Romeo may not best be impersonated by a woman'. On the other side of the Atlantic the *New York Times* of 1860 would in due course observe that 'there is in the delicacy of Romeo's character something which requires a woman to represent it, and unfits almost every man for its impersonation'.

But Romeo's comeback did not guarantee Juliet's. The part was played by Cushman's sister Susan, and we might have imagined that a family likeness between two female leading figures would restore something of the lost symmetry between the lovers. Contemporary images of the production tell another story, however. One shows Juliet looking upwards at a heroic Romeo, as if seeking reassurance. Another drawing of the Cushmans in the parting scene also portrays a Juliet who gazes up at her lover. His arms support her protectively, while his face is turned away as if to confront his destiny. *The Times* noted that Susan played the balcony scene with 'a beautifully confiding and truly feminine air', delighting the reviewer when, at the lines about whether Romeo's intentions were honourable, she hesitated with 'maiden-like modesty' before pronouncing the word 'marriage'.

On the stage, at least, the acknowledgement of Romeo's self-proclaimed effeminacy seems to have made Juliet still more fragile, preserving the contrast between the sexes. Meanwhile, Shakespeare's text was available in print and the success of the Bowdlers' *Family Shakespeare* testifies to the habit of reading the plays aloud round the fire. Unbowdlerized, Shakespeare's own Juliet offered a dangerous role model for young women, demonstrating a wilfulness that was not to be encouraged. Midnight conversations and secret assignations were out of order; marriage in defiance of parental choice might be romantic but it was also perilous. As early as 1775 in *The Morality of Shakespeare's Drama Illustrated* Elizabeth Griffith had treated the tragic outcome for the lovers as no more than poetic justice 'for their having ventured upon an unweighed engagement together, without the concurrence and consent of their parents'. Evidently, the cultural shift to marriage based on love did not do away with the requirement for family approval.

Death seems a high price to pay for disobedience but later moralists, including some proto-feminists, while they admired Juliet's staunch faithfulness and courage, and although they praised her artless devotion, were also uneasy about what they called her impulsiveness, irrationality, petulance. This was the great age of the realist novel – and character. What *sort of person*, the Victorians asked, would marry, against her parents' will, a man she had first met the night before? In his excellent book *Shakespeare and the Victorians* Adrian Poole reproduces John Gilbert's frontispiece to *Romeo and Juliet* in an edition of 1858. Kneeling at the feet of a stern but authoritative Capulet to plead against the marriage to Paris in 3.5, his daughter looks rebellious and sulky, while her pose echoes that of a naked, overtly sexual carving above her head. Juliet's independence was not acceptable – Victorian girls did as they were told.

By now, the parity Shakespeare depicted evidently made very little sense, although there were moments of resistance: William Hazlitt notably reprinted the whole of Juliet's epithalamion, on the grounds that it had no doubt been expunged from the Bowdlers' *Family Shakespeare*. (Perhaps he didn't know that that the theatre had expunged most of it long before that.) Some of the actresses also defended Juliet, though we might, I suppose, expect them to be partial. A brief note on the play, published in 1882 by Fanny Kemble, the Juliet of her time some half-century earlier, affirms that 'Romeo represents the *sentiment*, and Juliet the *passion* of love. The *pathos* is his, the *power* hers.' Writing a year earlier, Helena Faucit Martin, another star of the Victorian stage, finds much in Juliet to praise. She quotes the innocent parts of the wedding-night speech, describing Juliet's state of mind as 'joyful anticipation', without further comment. (Was she aware of the rest, even if it was habitually cut in performance?) She also quotes Shakespeare's final couplet as a fitting conclusion to the story. Even so, a neglected childhood has left the heroine unduly romantic, and 'To judge Juliet rightly', Faucit Martin concludes, 'we must have clear ideas of Romeo, of her parents, and of all the circumstances that determined her conduct'.

If the nineteenth century cannot escape the kind of reading required by the realist novel, the Victorians are also driven, it seems, by the obligation to make moral judgements. And for young women in this period morality is first and foremost sexual morality. The question the Victorians raise about the lovers concerns not equality but virtue and, however far her background may exonerate her, Juliet's behaviour is foolish or wrong, or perhaps both.

Modernity

Can we count on our own epoch to redeem the lovers from the opposition brought into being by post-Shakespearean stereotypes of gender and Victorian morality? Dominic Dromgoole's Globe production of 2009 went some way to restore the balance, but here the sheer strength and charm of a brilliant Romeo tended to overshadow Juliet. In gender terms, the two major films of the play seem to me disappointing to the degree that they substitute sentiment for passion.

First, while no one, surely, could fail to be charmed by Zeffirelli's rich, velvety film of 1968, his child-protagonists, faithful to the literal fact of Juliet's age, lack the stature of Shakespeare's central figures. Zeffirelli's neo-realism leads him to cut much of the heroic dialogue, including the anxiety of 2.2.116–20 and the reckless daring of Juliet's wedding-night speech. The film deletes the courage attached to drinking the potion, Juliet's punning defiance of her mother and her calm rebuttal of Paris's proprietary addresses; as her father storms in 3.5, Zeffirelli's Juliet cowers on the floor behind the Nurse's skirts. This love story is pretty, cute rather than grand. Visually, the symmetry between the lovers is restored but at the expense of the passion. More victims than protagonists, they are beautiful children, babes in the wood, their tale sad but not tragic.

In Baz Luhrmann's dazzling *William Shakespeare's Romeo + Juliet* nearly 30 years later, the central figures are fractionally older, slightly more sexually aware, and played by more accomplished performers. But Juliet's white fancy dress emphasizes her innocence: she is both the 'bright angel' (2.2.26) and the 'snowy dove' (1.5.47) of Shakespeare's text, as well as the dove of peace that flutters across the screen when the Friar imagines rancour dissolved by love (2.3.88). Her courageous potion speech is deleted. Meanwhile, Romeo's long hair and physical beauty, as well as his propensity to write poems, all isolate him from the other, more aggressively masculine Montague boys. Visually, once again, much of the symmetry between the lovers is preserved but here, too, without the grandeur. As in Zeffirelli's film, the text is cut to make way for the images and the love scenes, when they are not silent, are conducted in whispers. It is as if we need to know the words in advance in order to follow them. Since in the play the passion resides in the vocabulary and the imagery of the lovers' exchanges, their relegation to the background in the film simplifies the love story. Danger here comes from outside the protagonists; recklessness belongs to the fractured society, darkness to the self-indulgent nightlife of Verona Beach, without penetrating the world of the lovers. Romeo and Juliet themselves, by contrast, are highly lit and repeatedly purified ('new baptized', 2.2.50) by water. The setting of the final scene is no vault but a candlelit marriage bed that morphs into an altar, reducing the couple to the 'sacrifices' Capulet names at the end of the play – though not the screenplay.

In the cinema, images take the place of words. If Shakespeare's theatre names what it can't show, film shows what it needn't tell. Zeffirelli solves the problem of Juliet's description of the wedding-night by removing it altogether, while Luhrmann radically curtails it. Instead, both films linger over the couple waking up in bed, discreetly naked on white sheets. The effect is to replace the play's passionate imagining with innocence and vulnerability. To echo Fanny Kemble's terms, there is in the love stories these films depict more pathos than power.

Paradoxically, something of the play's gender-equality is restored on the screen in two adaptations that break more radically with the original. The heroine of *West Side Story* doesn't die. Instead, she takes authoritative possession of the gun that killed Tony and then, surprisingly, throws it to the ground, repudiating violence and shaming the warring gangs into a tentative reconciliation. Maria, who has stood throughout for peace, rises and follows the funeral procession, sorrowful but dignified.

Shakespeare in Love comes at the issue from a different angle. Here the screenplay is as important as the images in the backstage story of two rival houses, an impossible love threatened by an arranged marriage, and a friend's death in a brawl, all intimately linked with the onstage emergence of *Romeo and Juliet*. The lovers on and off stage are grown up. Viola defies the convention that forbids women to act, slaps the face of her proprietary bridegroom, and contradicts the Queen, who also knows something of what it is to be a woman in a man's profession, she confesses. On the stage Viola plays both lovers, first Romeo and then Juliet; in the love scenes between Will and Viola, even while the images insist on the difference between the sexes, Viola speaks Romeo's lines, Will Juliet's. At Will's 'What satisfaction canst thou have tonight?', 'That's my line', Viola protests. 'And mine too', its author justifiably replies. Eventually, Will plays Romeo to Viola's Juliet. Although it makes no attempt to reinstate symmetry in the original terms, the film insists on an interchangeability of gender that finds a parallel in the play. Without erasing the distinction between male and female, or playwright and heiress, *Shakespeare in Love* reconstructs in its own terms a reversibility in love that reaches back to *Romeo and Juliet*.

Violence

Shakespeare's play tells two stories: on the one hand, a tale of star-crossed love; on the other, the record of a motiveless feud that engulfs people who set out to play no part in it. The movies come into their own in their depiction of violence. This was a topic the twentieth century had reason to know a good deal about, but that realization registered only gradually in Western culture. By the 1990s it was possible to look back on two bitterly fought world wars, a racially motivated holocaust, and a succession of hard-won wars of independence, as well as any number of local conflicts where the sophistication of the weaponry allowed the death and mutilation of numbers unimaginable only a hundred years before. From 1945 to 1989 the world lived in conscious fear of nuclear extinction. Meanwhile, on the streets the availability of handguns meant disputes too easily turned deadly. And all this was literally brought home to us by the broadcast media.

In my view, the films mark an increasing cultural preoccupation with violence and its consequences. Cukor's film of 1936 shows the feud as primarily an affair of the younger generation. The first brawl is provoked by the clownish Peter, who then plays no further part in the scrum he has initiated. The adults join in only at the last moment and with some reluctance. This makes their final reconciliation more consonant with probability but diminishes the threat parental opposition represents for the lovers. *West Side Story* in 1961 also confines the hostility to the young: their parents are represented only by an offscreen voice and the tailors' dummies enlisted as witnesses to the 'wedding' in the bridal shop where Maria works. At the same time, the turf war is intense, pervasive and dangerous. In 1996, by contrast, Baz Luhrmann engages a whole society in the conflict: Verona Beach is fractured on commercial, racial and gender lines, and evidently beyond the reach of reconciliation. Montague and Capulet are rival companies; the Montagues are white, Juliet's father and the Capulet boys, including Tybalt, Latinos; law and order are represented by the African American Chief of Police, Captain Prince – and challenged by the anarchic, transvestite African American Mercutio. From the aggression of the opening sequence, culminating in the fire that burns down the Phoenix gas station (Shakespeare's 'The Phoenix and Turtle', anyone? Conventionally the phoenix dies in flames, to rise again from its own ashes), it is increasingly apparent that the social turmoil is uncontrollable. There are no joined hands at the end of this exhilarating, disturbing movie.

In the play, however, turbulence not only surrounds the lovers, it also inhabits their relationship itself. Passion, the text indicates, is characterized by sudden anxieties and 'violent delights' (2.6.9); love is reckless, like Phaeton and his out-of-control steeds; desire is invaded, I have argued in Chapter 3, by death. The turning point of the love story comes when Romeo kills Tybalt: the hero is not outside the fray but implicated in it, however reluctantly. And, as you will have discovered if you carried out the analysis I recommended at the end of Chapter 3, violence dominates the final scene. From the moment he arrives at the Capulet tomb, Romeo's intents are 'savage-wild'; he threatens to tear the unoffending Balthasar limb from limb; he is driven, he declares, by imperatives 'More fierce and more inexorable far / Than empty tigers or the roaring sea' (5.3.35–9). As he forces open the jaws of the monument, Romeo kills Paris, with whatever regret, for trying to impede him. Where the dispatch of Tybalt might be seen as the execution of a killer (3.1.187–8), the death of Paris is harder to justify. In the tomb Romeo dies flanked by the two corpses he himself has made.

When Zeffirelli and Luhrmann cut the fight with Paris, and Luhrmann also excludes Tybalt's body from the final scene, they sanitize the love story they tell. Romance becomes wholesome, if powerless in an unwholesome world. This was the preferred reading in the nineteenth century, too. A painting of 1853–5 by Frederic, Lord Leighton typifies the Victorian representation of the last scene. The mode is realism.

The dead Juliet in white embraces her prone husband's head; Paris in a red cloak sits slumped beside them. There is no sign of violence; if we didn't know better, we might think all three were sleeping. Lady Capulet has thrown herself on her daughter's body in elegant, silk-clad grief. Behind the lovers, the fathers shake hands under the supervision of the Prince, while the Friar appeals to heaven. This peaceable image implies a direct opposition between the love story and the feud. (The painting can be viewed at http://www.museumsyndicate.com/item.php?item=11992).

In *Shakespeare and the Victorians* Adrian Poole picks out a curious counter-example of 1870. By the standards of photographic realism that prevailed in orthodox circles, Ford Madox Brown's *Romeo and Juliet* is awkward to the point of eccentricity. But the Pre-Raphaelites challenged orthodoxy, habitually foreshortening distances and adopting unexpected viewing angles, with the effect of intensifying the emotion depicted. Brown's painting shows the lovers parting on the balcony where Juliet first declared her love. Romeo's left leg is precariously entangled in the rope ladder but not supported by it; his left arm is outstretched over thin air. Juliet clasps her departing lover in vain; her eyes are closed (in intense emotion, or to keep out the daylight that divides them?); Romeo's face is buried in her neck. If we turn the image on its side, we can already begin to see them as they were so often portrayed in the tomb. (The picture can be found as the first thumbnail at http://www.preraph.org/gallery/). An earlier version of 1867 can be seen at the Whitworth Art Gallery, Manchester.) Passion and danger are perceived as inseparable components of the moment, integral to the love story, not merely outside it.

Among the movies, it is *West Side Story* that most clearly complicates the idea of a simple antithesis between the lovers and a hostile world. 'Tonight' is first sung as a duet in the 'balcony scene' conducted on the fire escape, as Tony and Maria declare their love: 'Tonight, tonight / The world is full of light.' But the song is reprised when they look forward to their meeting after the rumble. This time it represents the film's reinscription of Juliet's address to the night: Maria laments that 'The minutes seem like hours / The hours go so slowly'. But meanwhile, the rival gangs are assembling, also in song: 'The Jets are gonna have their way – tonight'; 'The Sharks are gonna have their day – tonight.' Eventually, Anita, Tony, Maria, the Jets and the Sharks are all singing independently, their performances culminating simultaneously in the same word, 'tonight'. This conjunction of awaited joy and expected violence invests with intense irony Maria's concluding exhortation to the moon to 'make this endless day / Endless night'.

Genre

Shakespeare's play blends elements of realism with a grander, more heroic manner. This verse drama with moments of verisimilitude owes its iconic status to the poetic and lyrical exchanges between a couple who are elevated by this means above the individuals they *are*, representing instead all lovers for all time *as they might be*. Romeo and Juliet are rendered larger than life by their declarations of a love that is 'as boundless as the sea' (2.2.133), defying definition, in excess of any words that might convey it (2.6.33–4). The poetry slows down the action, inviting playgoers to reflect on the nature of the love it presents. Romeo and Juliet say what any lover might wish to have said, and at the same time insist on the inadequacy of that too, when it comes to defining a condition both representative and hard to name without falling into cliché. That is why Shakespeare's figures allow space for character readings; it is also why interpretations in terms of individual character will never do justice to the play.

The eighteenth-century adaptations, I have suggested, by curtailing the poetry, diminish the central figures and especially Juliet. Paradoxically, the period's deference to metrical regularity and consistently elevated diction steers

Shakespeare's daring eloquence towards a banality that is only compounded by the invention of passages of extra dialogue doomed to fall short of the original. Where we have the modified texts (Cibber's, Garrick's) it is possible to mark the difference of genre. In the nineteenth century, when we are more dependent on reviews of performances, however, especially in an epoch when character-impersonation is seen as the criterion of success, it is much more difficult to gauge how far past productions realized or, indeed, aspired to a Shakespearean grandeur.

In this respect, perhaps the films have most to offer us now as instances of adaptation that at once differ from the play and draw attention to its specific qualities. It is as if the process of transposition from stage to screen challenges directors to find another way to capture the combination of realism and the heroic they find in Shakespeare's text. For all the neo-realism of his characterization, Zeffirelli reinscribes the largeness of the verse in terms of visual art. While his teenage lovers are distinguished more by their charm than by their poetry, the film invokes Italian Renaissance painting, itself iconic for modern culture, as if in compensation. When, for example, Zeffirelli replaces the lamentations for Juliet's supposed death with a richly coloured funeral pageant, exactly as it might have been depicted at what many people perceive as the high point of Western art, the images defer the outcome in a way that parallels Shakespeare's heroic verse, blending the story with a larger tradition that invites the viewer to see beyond the immediacy of the individual lovers.

As a musical, *West Side Story* already allows for a conjunction of verisimilitude and formalization. In musicals song and dance routines commonly break with realism, arresting the story and resetting the characters inside a different convention. (An exception is the backstage musical, where the songs and dances are motivated by rehearsals or performances.) *West Side Story* exploits this tradition in a way that had not been seen before: there is no chorus; the dances, in particular, are not interludes but are integrated into the unfolding action, just as Shakespeare's verbal conceits are integral to the plot and yet delay events. *West Side Story* insists on the authenticity of its setting. Initially the Jets in the playground might be any group of local kids clicking their fingers in a menacing way. But as the rhythm intensifies and the choreography gradually becomes more mannered, more acrobatic, the nature of the feud is uncovered visually without recourse to words. The dances are extravagant, highly stylized and faultlessly executed – like Shakespearean rhetoric, perhaps.

Baz Luhrmann does something different – predictably. In *William Shakespeare's Romeo + Juliet*, hyper-realism allows viewers to have it both ways: the locations carry conviction; at the same time, they comment by exaggeration on the world they present. The giant concrete Christ constitutes the emblem of a religion that, however showy, or however benign, proves ultimately ineffectual. Meanwhile, insisting on a magnificence that is pompous, artificial or ruined, the settings work as verisimilitude, even while they also symbolize the proximity of wealth and decay. There is hectic action but – in Mercutio's cross-dressed performance, for instance, or in the encounter of the lovers through the fish tank – there is also much inventive stylization that slows down the plot.

At the same time, the film captures something of the variety of modes that defines Shakespeare's play (to the despair of his eighteenth-century revisers) from high poetry to low comedy, from wit to action, and back to tragedy. Luhrmann not only contrasts street violence and romance, as in *West Side Story*; he also invokes distinct visual modes in rapid succession, when the film switches from television newscast to action movie, to comedy with the nuns at the Phoenix, through spaghetti western close-ups and a bar-room shoot-out with oil cans, to Tybalt's ritualistic slow-motion gun-play. Like the tragedy, the film is also densely intertextual: its slogan-quotations work as conceits for us to enjoy, embedding the now-classic Shakespeare in the story, just as Shakespeare embeds classical mythology (Phaeton, Cynthia, Venus) in the play's present. And Luhrmann's imagery un-metaphorizes

Shakespeare's comparisons. If Juliet is shown as the angel/dove of Shakespeare's imagery, Paris, that 'precious book of love', who 'only lacks a cover' (1.3.88–9), now becomes a coverboy for *Time* magazine, while Romeo appears at the ball as Juliet's 'true knight' (3.2.142).

This is not, in my view, William Shakespeare's *Romeo + Juliet* but Baz Luhrmann's. And yet, in spite of that, or perhaps because of it, Baz Luhrmann's cinematic version brings out qualities of William Shakespeare's play that go a long way to justify the claim asserted by the title.

PS

After I finished this chapter, I sank back on the sofa to watch the first episode of an award-winning television western. Believe it or not, it showed *Romeo and Juliet* turning up in an unexpected place. *Hatfields and McCoys* concerns two feuding clans in the American South in the 1860s. Their children fall in love, but the families forbid them to marry. He has had previous sexual encounters; she hasn't; she has another suitor, approved by her kin. (Shakespeare is not mentioned.)

In the event this didn't lead anywhere very interesting, but *Warm Bodies* did (dir. Jonathan Levine, 2013). R is a zombie while Julie is alive; there's a nurse and a balcony scene. R eats Parry's brain, so the movie doesn't follow the original in every particular. And true love proves redemptive, as it so often does these days, which just goes to show how things have changed since 1595.

Whatever the variants, this story just won't go away.

Writing matters

There is probably no better way to come to terms with what is involved in adaptation than to do the work. Prepare a scene

(I suggest 1.5: the feast offers plenty of varied material) for production in any mode you like: stage performance, film, television, an opera, a painting, a western. Will your version aim at fidelity to Shakespeare's text? If so, explain what problems this presents in the twenty-first century. Will you cut the text, and if so, where and why? Or do you plan a radical reinscription of the play? If so, what is your object here? How do you intend to assert a difference, while retaining enough of the original to justify the view that your version belongs to the afterlife of Shakespeare's tragedy?

Decide on your setting and costume. Will you aim at sixteenth-century dress or adopt the clothes of some other period? If you choose modern dress, how does this change Shakespeare's play? Think about lighting and camera angles, if you like. How far will you differentiate between the characters in terms of their appearance and the way they speak? Block the scene: locate your actors from one moment to another and specify how they move in relation to each other.

In short, how will your version resemble Shakespeare's and how will it differ? What features of *Romeo and Juliet* will it single out for attention?

You might not get this question in an exam, but in the process of answering it you will discover a great deal about ways of seeing the play; you will also put yourself in an exceptionally strong position to analyze an existing adaptation.

Bear in mind that your writing will require some clarity and precision if you are to enable your reader (or yourself in six months' time) to visualize the details of your version, as well as to grasp the point of your contribution to the afterlife of the play. Do everything possible to bring what you say to life in a way that takes a reader with you.

CHAPTER SEVEN

Critical issues and the text

Interpretative choices

Even if you've never knowingly read a word of criticism, the choices critics make when they write about the play often enter into the prevailing consensus and, by this means, exert an influence on your own interpretation. Since I can't think of anything more tedious for me to write or you to read than a survey of current criticism of *Romeo and Juliet*, in this chapter I shall isolate issues that have recurred in recent discussions of the play. Like adapters, critics belong to a time and place; consciously or unconsciously, they choose a reading in the light of what they take for granted. But we don't have to follow their choices: we, too, are free to choose. Among recent assumptions two stand out as barely contested, so obvious that there is apparently very little to discuss: the play depicts adolescent love; Mercutio is gay. Although I shall put counter-arguments to both these readings, since these rarely get a hearing, my project is not so much to sway your thinking against them as to query foregone conclusions. When it comes to interpretation, there are always options.

In the last chapter I set out some of the choices that have been made for the purposes of performance. If you were directing the play on the stage now, you might interpret the text in the light of what would interest and engage modern audiences. Criticism, however, has broadly (but not invariably) concerned itself with how the play might have been understood in its own time. This involves history, and not least a history of meanings. As the story of performances indicates, key terms that recur in the play – *love*, *marriage*, *friendship* – undergo changes of emphasis at different epochs. Their resonances now may not be quite the same as they were then.

One school of thought, currently in retreat, prefers to see Shakespeare as a source of universal truths about human nature, adopting the obvious reading of Ben Jonson's eulogizing comment on his dead colleague and rival, 'He was not of an age, but for all time'. But there is another way to interpret this claim. Perhaps Shakespeare's writing was not confined to his own age *because* he was of it, because, in other words, his writings testify to certain subtle differences between his time and others, giving later epochs precious access to ways of being and feeling that no longer exist in any other form. Cultural meanings and values alter. We take for granted that times have changed when it comes to our own attitudes to Victorian proprieties. In the last chapter, I suggested that the early modern world was open, at least in fiction, to a utopian ideal of gender relations that became unintelligible to the Victorians. Friendship, love, and sexuality also have a history and we are able to trace a part of their story in the fiction of a vanished moment.

If so, the first choice critics make is whether, on the one hand, to look for their own image in Shakespeare or, on the other, to allow the past to indicate its difference from the present. We can, of course, do both. There are continuities, or we could not hope to make sense of the text; there are also discontinuities, or we could not recognize instances where directors or editors have *modernized* the play.

Adolescent love?

Juliet is not yet fourteen: fact (or as close to fact as it's possible to get in fiction). Directors, and film directors in particular, I have suggested, clinging to this one piece of solid information, and taking it that Romeo is no more than a year or two older, have put a great deal of stress on the adolescence of the central figures. Critics, following suit, have explained the extravagance of their romance as an effect of unruly hormones. By implication, grown-ups would experience love in some other way – more calmly and sensibly, perhaps, in line with the Friar's advice (2.6.14). The assumption is so widespread that it is not worth documenting. But is it well founded? And does it miss something that might matter?

The question is not whether Juliet is a couple of weeks short of fourteen – she is. The more pressing issue is what that age is taken to mean in the play, or whether we are invited to see teenage love as distinctive. Is the extravagance characteristic of youth, or of passion itself? The question brings into focus the processes of interpretation: in order to resolve it, what criteria do we use? What weight do we ascribe to existing criticism? How far should social and cultural history influence our sense of how the events enacted on the stage might have been understood by early modern audiences?

Where, in short, do we look for arguments and evidence? First and foremost, the text, of course. The play depicts more than one attitude to the implications of Juliet's age. In the first instance, there is her father's view:

> My child is yet a stranger in the world;
> She hath not seen the change of fourteen years.
> Let two more summers wither in their pride
> Ere we may think her ripe to be a bride. (1.2.8–11)

Capulet evidently thinks her too young to marry – but only by two years. Nearly 16 would be fine, it seems. Paris counters,

'Younger than she are happy mothers made' (12). As a man in a hurry, he has an axe to grind – but Capulet does not dispute the proposition. Instead, he makes a grumbling appeal to the proverbial wisdom: 'And too soon marred are those so early married' (13).

At this point the audience has not yet seen Juliet herself. It is as if the play is setting up a plausible context for its action, the father predictably hesitant to part with what he perceives as his little girl, the suitor equally reluctant to wait. But is it at the same time an imaginary context, a fictional Italy where they do things differently? Perhaps. When Capulet's wife broaches the topic with a surprised Juliet, she confirms Paris's comment:

> Younger than you,
> Here in Verona, ladies of esteem,
> Are made already mothers. By my count,
> I was your mother much upon these years
> That you are now a maid. (1.3.70–4)

After making a quick calculation of Lady Capulet's present age (an almost irresistible impulse, surely?), an audience might notice that she is telling them, in effect, that this is how things are generally done *in Verona*; this is what marriage means here. The strategy is familiar to us from historical novels or science fiction: in what they say the characters create for the reader specific meanings that define the unfamiliar world they inhabit.

It is 'ladies of esteem' who marry young, and the social history of the early modern period indicates that marital habits in Verona would not, after all, have seemed so very eccentric in Shakespeare's London. The legal age of marriage for girls was 12 (14 for boys). Most couples married much later than this, but then most couples had to save enough money to establish a separate household and prepare to support unknown numbers of children (no small consideration in an age without effective contraception). However, where money was no object, wives might be very young. There were no English royal marriages in Elizabeth I's time but Princess Anna of Denmark was fourteen in 1589, when she married King James VI of Scotland, later James I of England. (She did not become a mother, however, until five years later.) Frances Walsingham, daughter and heir of Elizabeth's Secretary of State, married Sir Philip Sidney in 1583, when she was 16. Paris is a man of 'fair demesnes' and 'noble parentage' (3.5.180–81); Capulet is 'rich' (2.3.54, 1.5.116). Early marriage, Juliet's mother indicates, marks high status.

According to much fiction of the period, love was for the young and was treated with some indulgence by their elders. In *As You Like It* Jaques mocks it as the third of his seven ages of man: first, the infant, next the schoolboy (roughly from seven to fourteen at that time), 'then the lover, / Sighing like furnace, with a woeful ballad / Made to his mistress' eyebrow' (2.7.148–50). Maintaining the preceding intervals, this would place the lover between 14 and 21, and other literary sources confirm this period as the appropriate age of for young men to fall in love. In 1600 the essayist William Cornwallis patronizes the condition as 'a very fine thing, the badge of eighteen and upward'.

Poetic convention did not necessarily associate such love with marriage. Any number of lyrics of the epoch urge the young to make love now, while their years allow, since beauty is like the morning dew; time flies, and flowers wither; 'Youth's a stuff will not endure' (*Twelfth Night*, 2.3.52). But for the women it was primarily addressed to, this might be rash counsel. Juliet is right to fear that this sudden love may not survive (2.2.118–20). Laertes warns his sister Ophelia not to risk her honour or her chastity in response to Hamlet's overtures (*Hamlet*, 1.3.29–44), but to regard his young love as 'A violet in the youth of primy nature, / Forward, not permanent, sweet, not lasting' (7–8).

There is some further evidence of an idea of adolescence for boys. 'I would there were no age between ten and three-and-twenty', grumbles the old Shepherd in *The Winter's Tale*, 'for there is nothing in the between but getting wenches with child, wronging the ancientry, stealing, fighting' (3.3.59–63). I have found no such evidence for girls, who were probably less free – and less inclined? – to practise anti-social behaviour. *Love* in such a context means a transitory condition, youthful, lyrical, delightful, intense, perhaps absurd, possibly dangerous, that might or might not be reliable or serious.

At the same time, in another and contradictory area of early modern culture, love was fast becoming the only proper basis for marriage. While many elite unions (involving ladies of esteem) were still, in practice, arranged to ensure the dynastic transmission of property, the clergy on the one hand and fiction on the other were newly promoting the ideal of marrying for love. Shakespeare's comedies played a part in this process. While love might be seen in poetry as a passing phase, the institution of marriage was permanent, and the loving family was coming to be seen as a microcosm of social life and a seminary of good subjects. Once married, both men and woman of any age were adult citizens, responsible for inculcating in their children the values of their society. *Romeo and Juliet* dramatizes the fault line between dynastic and loving alliances. In establishing that their bent of love is honourable, their purpose marriage (2.2.143–4), Romeo and Juliet raise their love to a new level.

Morality

A generation ago, criticism often saw itself as a source of pious instruction. Fiction was supposed to illustrate a moral truth or deliver a worthy message. Texts were reducible in the last analysis to fables, or to conduct books masquerading as stories. Like the Victorian writings I cited in Chapter 6, such criticism could not resist the imperative to judge. And like the eighteenth century, it often maintained a strong attachment to the idea of poetic justice. If events went badly, someone had failed to reach the highest moral standard. To maintain poetic justice, plays with unhappy endings were held to invest their protagonists with a 'tragic flaw'.

One highly valued quality at this time was 'maturity': maturity was everything the critic endorsed; immaturity was deplorable. To qualify as mature, or to mature in the course of the play, characters in Shakespeare were repeatedly required to learn moral lessons. An insistence that the protagonists of *Romeo and Juliet* were adolescents explained why things went wrong. This was their tragic flaw. Juliet was not yet fourteen; they were no more than teenagers; small wonder they were prone to excesses of feeling and extravagant poetry; it was no surprise, so the story went, that they turned out to be rash, precipitate and, in the end, suicidal. Some critics, generously looking for signs of redemption, found evidence that Juliet matured in the course of the five days of the play; others located the tragedy in the death of young people who would never have the opportunity to learn the lesson of moderation and achieve the prized maturity.

Difference

Mercifully, we are now less judgmental, and more ready to attend to the possibility that the play, as the product of the sixteenth century, might not be dedicated to the affirmation of eighteenth- and nineteenth-century values. Love is for the young in early modern culture and yet, for all that, passion may strike at any age, and it remains just as extravagant in people who, according to the moralistic critics, should presumably know better. Othello is 'declined / Into the vale of years' when he tells Desdemona, 'I do love thee! and when I love thee not / Chaos is come again' (*Othello*, 3.3.269–70, 91–2). Cleopatra is 'wrinkled deep in time', she says, when the news that Antony is dying prompts her to a grand cosmic comparison: 'O sun / Burn the great sphere thou mov'st in!

Darkling stand / The varying shore o'th' world!' (*Antony and Cleopatra*, 1.5.30; 4.15.10–12).

If such grown-up love was just as prone to excess, it was also equally capable of recklessness. As these examples indicate, there was in the fiction of the period nothing specifically adolescent about dying for love. Age does not make Othello or Antony and Cleopatra too wise to kill themselves. True, the immediate classical prototypes for Romeo and Juliet are young lovers, Pyramus and Thisbe (2.4.42), whose sad story is turned to farce by incompetent actors in *A Midsummer Night's Dream*. Supposing Thisbe dead, Pyramus kills himself; finding Pyramus dead, Thisbe takes her own life with his sword. But Virgil's Dido (2.4.41), theme of a recent play by Christopher Marlowe and another constant point of reference for Shakespeare's own texts, was already a queen and a widow when she killed herself with the sword of Aeneas on the bonfire she had built to burn the belongings he had left behind.

Genre again

Perhaps Francis Bacon saw some of Shakespeare's tragedies. In any case, he had no patience with love: he viewed it as dangerous and damaging, calling it 'the child of folly'. And yet his observations may contribute more than he knew to an understanding of *Romeo and Juliet*'s appeal. 'The stage', he maintained, 'is more beholding to love than the life of man.' Plays, in other words, owe more, are more indebted, to romantic love than is real life. Bacon's main object is to denigrate love as an invention of the poets, with the theatre as the principal financial beneficiary, and he goes on to note the propensity of lovers to speak 'in a perpetual hyperbole'. His comment may be hostile, but doesn't it also point to precisely the feature of Shakespeare's play that differentiates it from life? The hyperbolic love scenes, which are not realism, where the characters address each other in verse and in inflated images, *stage* love in its most poetic incarnation, extricate it from the everyday, elevate it for contemplation and inscribe its contradictions. The lyric poetry of the play exchanges action for a succession of freeze-frames that make love available for inspection as irresistible but dangerous, at once courageous and reckless, high-risk because unconditional.

Bacon's comment indicates that this would have been more obvious then than it is now in an age of realism, when our drama is widely expected to reproduce the banality of actual dialogue. 'Every other night, on TV', Roland Barthes points out in *A Lover's Discourse*, 'someone says: *I love you*'. This deeply personal declaration is also a platitude. '*I love you*', Pascal Bruckner reaffirms in *The Paradox of Love*, 'the most intimate in the grip of the most anonymous'. The phrase, so deeply longed for, sought after, prized, belongs to any number of virtuous situations – and covers a multitude of sins. It cements a lifelong partnership, or pleads for a repetition in response, neatly concludes a phone call to your mum, initiates a heartless seduction, or denies an infidelity. In all these instances it serves to deflect questions. This statement, Barthes proposes, is without nuances: 'It suppresses explanations, adjustments, degrees, scruples.' Saying everything, as well as nothing in particular, it is therefore empty, enigmatic: what do you *mean* when you say you love me? A performative, the promise of something beautiful, the most precious utterance is also formulaic, second-hand, strangely blank.

Romeo and Juliet do not say 'I love you', and when Leonardo mouths the words to Claire in *William Shakespeare's Romeo + Juliet*, the effect is oddly mawkish. Romeo can do, has done, better than this. Shakespeare's language in the play rises above the commonplace to acknowledge the intensity and complexity of an emotion that at any age is glorious, engulfing, all-consuming, sometimes absurd, and potentially deadly. The distinctiveness, if any, of teenage love does not seem to me to be the play's main concern.

Artlessness

And yet the emphasis on Juliet's age remains a puzzle, not least because Shakespeare has altered his sources. In William Painter's narrative, she is nearly eighteen, in Arthur Brooke's *Romeus and Juliet* just sixteen. Both source stories raise the question of age only incidentally, when Juliet's parents discuss their daughter's sorrow, which they at first ascribe to Tybalt's death. They worry that Juliet does nothing but lament and shuts herself in her chamber without eating or drinking. But the cause must be more than the loss of her cousin; there is something she is not telling them, her mother surmises. It is probably that she wants to be married; surely she envies her married contemporaries, 'Whilst only she unmarried doth lose so many years' (*Romeus and Juliet,* line 1846). Perhaps, her mother goes on, Juliet fears that her parents mean to keep her from marriage forever. Capulet, ready to see the wisdom of this apparent insight, sets about finding Juliet a husband. (The echo of this conversation in the play is Lady Capulet's assumption that Juliet will welcome the news of her projected marriage to Paris, 3.5.107–15.) Her mother's guess is wrong but, ironically, not as far wrong as might at first appear. Like her friends of the same age, Brooke's Juliet *is* married, though secretly; she was indeed ready to marry months before.

What, then, are we to make of Shakespeare's emphatic alteration of his sources? It is tempting to pose the 'why' question and critics often do. 'Why does Shakespeare reiterate that Juliet is not yet fourteen?' But it is best not to yield to temptation. Such a question can have no available answer: we can't look inside Shakespeare's head. Perhaps it just seemed to him to work.

But we can usefully ask *how* it works, how Juliet's reduced age affects the story the audience is invited to engage with. In the first instance, it renders her more vulnerable to the demands of her parents and makes her resistance to forced marriage the more heroic. Capulet's threat to turn her out on the streets to 'hang, beg, starve, die' (3.5.193) is surely unforgiveable at any age, but Juliet's youth throws into relief the pathos of her plight. It would be a hard-hearted audience that shared the Victorian respect for obedience on these terms.

The younger the heroine, the deeper the conflict between the generations and the more intense the pity of the tragedy. It is worth noting that the romances which lead to happy endings in Shakespeare are often facilitated by parental absence: Beatrice lives with her uncle, Rosalind's father is thought to be to be missing in the forest, while Viola's is dead. These protagonists are self-determining, while Juliet is shown at the mercy of a family and a wider community. In *A Midsummer Night's Dream*, thematically and chronologically closest of the comedies to *Romeo and Juliet*, the happy ending relies on a heavy father overruled by a benign Duke. In the tragedy Juliet herself asserts what little sovereignty she possesses when she takes her own life rather than remarry (or enter a convent) under duress.

Second, her youth also confirms her artlessness. She has not thought of marriage (1.3.67); she has never been in love before and her responses are ingenuous, the outcome of true love, not practice. As Juliet herself knows, the early modern courtship process is, or ought to be, long and difficult. When she innocently bids farewell to convention (2.2.89), Juliet willingly surrenders the succession of visits and serenades, the gifts and flattery, the coaxing and cajoling, and the coy refusals that might be the material of a different play. The sonnet sequences full of rare comparisons that Romeo might be expected to compose are telescoped into a single sonnet in dialogue between a pilgrim and a saint (1.5.92–105). And from then on the play is effectively free to dramatize what I take to be its central concern, namely, passion in good times and bad.

Emphasis on the adolescence of Romeo and Juliet effectively focuses the play on teenage excess; the alternative is a tragedy of love's own extremes. Which do you prefer?

A gay Mercutio?

Reviewers began to detect a homoerotic Mercutio in the 1973 production of the play by Terry Hands for the Royal Shakespeare Company. The date is not entirely accidental. For many years sexual acts between men were illegal in the UK, punishable by imprisonment or, in the appalling case of Alan Turing in 1952, 'chemical castration'. Turing was required to take female hormones; he committed suicide in 1954. But in 1967 new legislation decriminalized sex in private between consenting males over 21 (it had never been illegal for women). This was not yet full equality: the heterosexual age of consent was 16; 'privacy' was subject to extremely stringent definition. But it was a huge step forward and the campaign for equal treatment of homosexuality would continue in a new atmosphere. To identify Mercutio as gay was a political choice as well as a textual one; it recruited an attractive fictional ally in a just campaign. The reviewers' perception was rooted, in other words, in its historical and cultural moment.

The classic critical case appeared in 1988 in Joseph A. Porter's *Shakespeare's Mercutio*. This book gives a new prominence to the play's most anarchic, phallic figure. Porter proposes a strongly suggestive line of descent from the eloquent, lawless god Mercury, while also invoking the liquid metal, mercury: Mercutio – mercurial – winged messenger – quicksilver. Strangely enough, however, the handful of allusions to Mercutio's homosexuality in Porter's book are relatively incidental, and based on assumptions rather than arguments. Certainly, Mercutio talks a lot about pricks, but if all young men who did that were gay, the world would soon be unpeopled.

Perhaps in Porter's American context reticence was still judicious. But if so, it proved no bar to Jonathan Goldberg's much stronger statement in 1994. Goldberg dwells on Mercutio's interest in Rosaline's open arse and Romeo's poperin pear (2.1.38). He argues that Rosaline takes a place in Romeo's poetic addresses parallel to that of the young man in Shakespeare's Sonnets. On the basis of the structural masculinity ascribed by this means to Rosaline, Goldberg maintains that, when Mercutio conjures Romeo's 'spirit' to 'stand / Till she had laid it and conjured it down' (24–6), he is obliquely offering himself as Romeo's sexual partner.

> The locus of anal penetration, of course, is available to any body, male or female. Mercutio's conjuring also conjures him into the magic circle, an O that that is not, as most commentators would have it be, the vaginal opening, for this is how Mercutio voices – through Rosaline – his desire for Romeo.

The full case involves a good deal of fancy interpretative footwork, and you would be well advised to read the essay before arriving at a judgement. But it is possible to endorse the politics of Goldberg's wish to enlist so engaging a figure as the witty, fluent, heroic Mercutio, while at the same time finding the textual argument somewhat strained.

Nevertheless, many commentators have gone on to take for granted that Shakespeare's Mercutio is simply and unequivocally gay. According to Goldberg, Tybalt accuses Mercutio of being 'Romeo's consort'. That isn't quite what Tybalt says: 'Mercutio, thou consortest with Romeo' (3.1.44). A consort (noun, Goldberg's modern English) is a settled sexual partner, a spouse; to 'consort with' (verb, Shakespeare's early modern English) defines a less specific and more transitory state of affairs, meaning anything from 'hang out with' to (conjecturally) 'practise sex with'. It is not entirely clear whether this is to be understood as a homophobic slur on Tybalt's part; either way, Mercutio roundly rejects the imputation – or perhaps simply its pomposity in the mouth of this 'antic, lisping, affecting fantastico' (2.4.28–9), pretending to interpret it with reference to a consort of musicians (45–8). There are no particular grounds for connecting musicians with homosexuality: sex plays no obvious part in their knockabout with Peter in 4.5. But Goldberg's phrase has stuck. The essay on the play in *Shakesqueer* in 2011 has Mercutio offended by 'Tybalt's suggestion that he is Romeo's consort' – and then appears to take Tybalt's word for it over Mercutio's.

History

The *Shakesqueer* reading explains Mercutio's resistance by reference to the punishment of sodomy at that time by death. It is true that early modern England defined sodomy as an abominable crime deserving execution. It is also true that very few people were ever prosecuted for it and, when they were, even fewer were found guilty. Much of the case for Mercutio's homosexuality depends on the presumption of a subtext in the play. In other words, it takes for granted the existence in the period of a love that dared not speak its name and was therefore obliged to communicate obliquely by hints and indirections. In practice, at the time of *Romeo and Juliet* society seems to have been relatively relaxed about the gender of objects of desire. Homoeroticism was not endorsed but neither did it generate hysteria. In his excellent *Impersonations*, Stephen Orgel argues that it was perceived as less dangerous than the love of women. Far from reluctant to speak, moreover, same-sex love proved remarkably voluble in Christopher Marlowe's *Edward II* (?1592), the poems of Richard Barnfield (1594, 1595), not to mention Shakespeare's Sonnets themselves, probably written in the 1590s. True, Edward II came to a nasty end, but in the play the main complaint about his love for the upstart Gaveston is that it distracts him from affairs of state, not that its object is a man. Ten years later, after the accession of James I in 1603, the king's predilection for handsome young men was an open secret but, again, the distaste this elicited seems to have owed more to the power he allotted them regardless of merit than to the sexual implications.

As in the case of the parity between Romeo and Juliet, what the fiction of the time can tell us, if we let it, is that this was a different cultural dispensation, in some ways more repressive than our own and in other ways less so. Michel Foucault radically changed our understanding of the past when he argued in *The History of Sexuality*, translated into English in 1978, that the category of homosexuality was constituted in the Victorian period and not before. Foucault, himself gay and committed to equality, pointed out that, whatever people did or did not do in the past, their actions did not confer an identity. That you *practised* this or that behaviour might make you guilty before the law, but it did not in consequence make you this or that *kind of person*.

> As defined by the ancient civil or canonical codes, sodomy was a category of forbidden acts; their perpetrator was nothing more than the juridical subject of them. The nineteenth-century homosexual became a personage, a past, a case history, and a childhood ... Nothing that went into his total composition was unaffected by his sexuality. It was everywhere present in him: at the root of all his actions because it was their insidious and indefinitely active principle; written immodestly on his face and body because it was a secret that always gave itself away. It was consubstantial with him, less as a habitual sin than as a singular nature ... The sodomite had been a temporary aberration; the homosexual was now a species.

It was the science of sexuality, Foucault maintained, that created sexual identities and, we might want to say, in the process constructed the closet. Coming out of the closet, while imperative if gay, lesbian, bisexual, and transgender allegiances are to achieve full recognition, does not substantially challenge the nineteenth-century classification. Can we be sure that laying emphatic claim to a single, given sexual identity, and one perceived as essential to who we are, does not close off some possibilities, even while it releases others? Desire does not always press in a single direction. In my view, given the right circumstances, it can go anywhere.

Foucault's historical analysis has generally been accepted as authoritative. In this light, perhaps we need to bring more nuances to our account of Mercutio. Whatever actors and directors may quite legitimately do to make the play relevant now, critics should probably give primacy to the text of the play. Subtexts and backstories may aid performance, and often generate magnificent theatre, but criticism has a different task to accomplish, giving primacy to what the play does say over what it doesn't. (There is a special Machereyan category of what *cannot* be said at a given time, but Pierre Macherey wanted us to see that as a gap or inconsistency in the culture of the period, not a secret that could be conveyed in winks and nudges.) The problem is that, while Mercutio's jokes about sexual organs have the effect of throwing into relief by contrast the romantic character of the heterosexual love story, they do not obviously single him out from other lads then and, indeed, now.

All criticism has a context. As I write, the majority of the British population favour gay marriage, which is on its way to legality. Fourteen other countries have already introduced it. What a transformation in less than half a century! Only a sceptic – a latter-day Mercutio, perhaps – would point out that the incorporation of gay, lesbian, and transgender people into this most respectable of institutions risks stripping these groups of their potential for subversion, while helping to prop up an institution heterosexuals are in the process of deserting. In such a climate, perhaps we can now afford to relax about the question of Mercutio's sexual orientation, if any? On the other hand, in many cultures various forms of fundamentalism continue to license the condemnation and punishment of homosexual acts. Such contexts are sure to inflect readings of the play, for better or worse.

Friendship

One of the most interesting features of Joseph Porter's book must be his discussion of the conflict between love and friendship in the play. He places Romeo at the centre of a struggle between Mercutio and Juliet, figures who do not encounter one another but are set in opposition to each other by the structure of the play. This conflict is decisive for the plot. Love makes Romeo reluctant to fight his bride's cousin, leaving the task, as Mercutio perceives it, to his friend; love (or is it friendship?) causes Romeo to intervene fatally in the encounter between them. Friendship makes Romeo avenge Mercutio's death (3.1.112), turning him into a killer and determining his banishment. The death of Mercutio at the midpoint of the play (3.1), bringing love and friendship into direct confrontation, forms the hinge that joins the potential comedy of the first half with the tragedy of the second.

We may therefore see Romeo poised between two alternatives. Juliet promises passion, Mercutio comradeship. Mercutio loses out, but not for want of trying. At his first appearance in 1.4, Mercutio does what he can to tease Romeo out of the unrequited devotion to Rosaline that is making him such a poor companion, concluding with the Queen Mab speech, a flight of comic eloquence that mocks the lover's immersion in dreams and fantasies. After the feast, he 'conjures' Romeo to rejoin the lads (2.1) but in vain: 'He jests at scars that never felt a wound' (2.2.1), Romeo comments. (If Mercutio is in love, his friend evidently hasn't noticed.) When a more convivial Romeo returns from a happier romantic meeting to exchange quips with his fellows, Mercutio supposes him cured and is delighted:

> Why, is this not better now than groaning for love? Now art thou sociable, now art thou Romeo, now art thou what thou art, by art as well as by nature, for this drivelling love is like a great natural [a fool] that runs lolling up and down to hide his bauble in a hole. (2.4.85–9)

Does that sound like an invitation to Romeo to hide his bauble in a different hole, or rather a contempt for the whole stupid business of love? The theme of Mercutio's witticisms seems to me to define the nature of Romeo's choice between a male scepticism on the one hand and an idealizing love on the other. But where there is contrast, there is also resemblance: the recklessness that characterizes both love and friendship leads to tragedy.

Perhaps the greatest threat to Mercutio's hopes, had he been alive to hear them, lies in Juliet's words to the departing Romeo: 'Art thou gone so, love, lord, ay husband, *friend*' (my emphasis; 3.5.43). The emergent cultural value of loving marriage changed the terms of the relationship between the couple. Partners were now friends too; a spouse was beginning to take up most of the emotional space available. Medieval chivalry had put a high premium on relations between men; a loyal companion could be relied on to help a warrior off the battlefield and send for a surgeon. And in peace a friend was there to share good news and bad. In Francis Bacon' s words, 'this communicating of a man's self to his friend works two contrary effects; for it redoubleth joys, and cutteth griefs in halfs'. Cornwallis went further. As sceptical towards romance as Mercutio, he maintained that real love could exist only between people of the same sex, since relationships between men and women were contaminated by desire. Stories in wide circulation in the sixteenth century, but now remembered only by cultural historians, celebrated the model friendships between men: Titus and Gisippus, Damon and Pithias.

But if medieval elite couples once entered into arranged marriages and spent their days in separate chambers, each with a same-sex retinue of knights or ladies in waiting, early modern married couples increasingly expected to be companions and friends, as well as lovers. To the degree that she too is Romeo's friend, Juliet unwittingly supplants Mercutio. As the meaning of marriage changed, the friendships outside it were gradually downgraded. Even now, something of the old tension remains: it is impossible to be simultaneously out with the boys (or girls) and at home with the family; marriage challenges prior practices.

The issue, it seems, was pressing in the early modern period, as the new meaning of marriage was brought into focus, not least by Shakespeare's plays. In an observant chapter of his book, Porter draws attention to Mercutio's phantom brother, Valentine, listed among the guests to be invited to the Capulet feast (1.2.67) and never heard of again. Has Valentine perhaps strayed into *Romeo and Juliet* from another play also set in Verona, where the protagonists are two gentlemen divided by love for Silvia? There, to preserve their amity, Valentine – very oddly to modern eyes – offers Silvia to his friend Proteus. *The Two Gentlemen of Verona*, probably first performed in the early 1590s, opens with Valentine teasing a Proteus he sees as rendered absurd by love:

> Love is your master, for he masters you;
> And he that is so yoked by a fool,
> Methinks should not be chronicled for wise. (1.1.39–41)

(Bacon subscribes to the same view, quoting with approval a saying that it is impossible to love and be wise.) Valentine's register is too polite to include baubles and holes but the sentiments resemble Mercutio's. Nor would this play be the end of the story. In *The Merchant of Venice*, a year or two after *Romeo and Juliet*, Portia sets up a struggle for Bassanio's wedding ring between his bride and the young lawyer who saves the life of his friend Antonio. If this contest is easily resolved, the imperative to incorporate Antonio into the marital rejoicing at the end of the play is presented as less comic.

Once we embark on this train of thought, the way-stations increase. Isn't *Love's Labour's Lost* intelligible in terms of a conflict between love on the one hand and loyalty to the same-sex group on the other? This play is usually dated a year or two earlier than *Romeo and Juliet*. Nor are women excluded from the rival claims of love and friendship. Hermia and Helena, close childhood companions, quarrel over love in *A Midsummer Night's Dream*. In *Much Ado About Nothing* (1598–9) Beatrice poses a dilemma for Benedick when she urges him to prove he loves her by killing his friend to avenge her friend and cousin. As late as 1613–14 *Two Noble Kinsmen* revisits the issue when it dramatizes Chaucer's tale of Palamon and Arcite, classic instance of a friendship turned to antagonism by love.

Our own culture is deeply sexualized. Alan Bray, one of the best historians of both homosexuality and friendship, urges us to recognize the difference of the past: 'The inability to conceive of relationships in other than sexual terms says something of contemporary poverty.' In early modern culture close relations between people of the same sex were highly prized, widely idealized, and at the same time shown in fiction as likely to conflict with love. But what exactly did such friendships mean? At this distance of time, it is surely impossible to recover the exact limits of comradeship as it was understood in the period. Who is now to say what exchanges between friends were acceptable in moments of intimacy? Shakespeare presents the relationship between Mercutio and Romeo as predominantly playful. In the course of one verbal contest, Mercutio offers to bite his friend's ear in acknowledgement of a good joke (2.4.76). This threat – or promise – is evidently made in sport.

To do justice to the past, we should treat its traces tactfully and with delicacy. If desire can go anywhere, it seems more than possible that playfulness included an element of homoeroticism. On the evidence of this text I personally would be reluctant to commit myself further. How about you?

Writing matters

I have concentrated on these two issues, the implications of Juliet's age and Mercutio's relationship with Romeo, both because they seem to me current and because they are exemplary for criticism. They call into play, in other words, most of the criteria we bring to bear, consciously or unconsciously, when we undertake a critical reading of any text. Criticism, I have suggested, differs from performance in that it delivers a distinct kind of knowledge. Performance may or may not have responsibilities to the past; it certainly has obligations to the present. Criticism, by contrast, is always undertaken in the present and will be influenced by its own moment. But its first responsibility is to the past in its difference; it can tell us something (not everything) about how the play works but also about the distinct cultural moment that generated a specific crystallization of the meanings and values then in circulation. And this matters because it opens up options. The way things are now is not always inevitable, not so much a fact of nature as the effect of culture and subject to history.

Any number of examination questions may put in front of you other issues that arise in the play, followed by an injunction to 'Discuss'. Rather than address them here, you might like to make explicit, as a final exercise, the criteria you believe we should invoke when we approach such a discussion. What are we looking for when we attempt to make sense of a text? Are there any limits on interpretation? What are the sources of information good criticism appeals to? What makes one critical argument more convincing than another? How important to the critic, in order of priority, are the text, the past and the present? And what reservations do we need to take into account when we invoke all three?

If you can do that for this play, with a view to putting your criteria to work in specific instances, there is in Shakespeare criticism or, indeed, in English – or drama studies, or cultural criticism – nothing you *can't* do from now on.

CHAPTER EIGHT

Writing skills

The project

Writing is a craft like any other. It owes something, no doubt, to nature (Shakespeare seems to have an edge that is hard to account for in any other way) but it's more to indebted to reflection and hard work (Shakespeare improved exponentially with practice, if Sonnet 145 was really written, as many believe, when he was no more than 18. Read it and compare the play!).

The first imperative is to consider what you want to achieve. What, in other words, is the object of the exercise? Most of the time, to appease an assessor, if we're honest, but there is an incidental advantage to be gained on the way, which is that writing induces you to find out what you think. Writing requires us to crystallize our interpretations, as vague sympathies and cloudy intuitions take shape in the form of readings and arguments. I include myself here: you'd be surprised how much I've discovered about how I see *Romeo and Juliet* in the course of writing this book.

As far as the appeasement process is concerned, the key is to elicit the assessor's respect. As I've done my best to indicate, there are different opinions on almost every aspect of the play. You have (or will find you have) views, and it can't be taken for granted that these will coincide with your reader's. (Better if they don't entirely, I'd say, if you want your work to be interesting.) Persuade him or her to see it your way. If you bear in mind that you're setting out to coax a reader to share your point of view, almost everything else follows. But just for the record, here are some of the ways to do it.

Clarity

If readers are to be persuaded to share your position, they need to know what it is. That's not as simple as it sounds, given that we often don't know in detail what we think till we see what we write. For that reason, give it time. Never, *ever* start the night before the deadline. You've got away with it so far? Well, then, just think how brilliantly you could have done with more time and attention.

Write early and write often. You can afford to assemble the parts of the argument you're sure of, on the assumption that you can adapt them later to fit in. The first attempt doesn't usually do justice to the subtleties – that takes a while. Meanwhile, declutter: such phrases as *it is the case that* and *in a very real sense* don't do any work. Delete them ruthlessly. Write and rewrite, polish and smooth. Above all, clarify, and then clarify some more.

Specifically, be lucid. Avoid convoluted formulations and tangled sentences. How can readers be persuaded if they can't confidently pick their way through your syntax? Be sure to explain whatever needs to be explained in order to convince your reader. You may need to locate an episode or a speech. If so, do it briskly, without rehearsing the whole plot. Quote if and when you plan to say something about the passage you're quoting, but not to save yourself the effort of summarizing or paraphrasing.

You are making a case. You may want to take account of the opposite case, or even make concessions to it, but in the end you are putting forward a view. Whatever it is, make sure that the argument (not the plot, for instance) determines the relationship between one paragraph and the next. A good trick is to check that the first sentence of each paragraph makes a point that the rest of it will substantiate. And organize the argument in such a way that the reader always knows what point you are making and how it contributes to the overall argument.

Authority

Don't run the risk of being dismissed as incompetent or (horror) infantile. This means following the conventions of formal written exchange. They *are* no more than conventions, but they will make your reader feel at home and relaxed – ready, in other words, to pay attention to your argument rather than your erratic punctuation. Computers can largely be trusted to sort out your spelling but they're less reliable when it comes to semi-colons. Own a simple paperback book on punctuation, with examples, and read it to see what freedom can be yours when you command the heights.

Be accurate. Your reader can probably be counted on to know the play, perhaps well. Check every quotation and every reference for accuracy: don't risk irritating the person you want to convince.

Fluency

It's amazing how persuasive fluency can be. English is a rich and wonderful resource and there's every reason to take full advantage of its capabilities. It never ceases to puzzle me that so many of my colleagues, who spend their lives in the company of the most eloquent writers, seem content to regale their own readers with the most dismal prose.

Academic writing produces some real ear-clouters (a term I gratefully borrow from Martin Amis). I'll confine myself to denouncing one current instance, the unaccountable preference for the ponderous passive (*is indicative of, is suggestive of,* even *is revelatory of*). Shakespeare would turn in his grave. Active verbs are much more compelling: *indicates, suggests, reveals.*

Useful practices include not repeating the same word too often (my besetting sin), not beginning too many sentences with the same word (usually *The*), and varying the length of the sentences themselves. Select the precise term. Use a dictionary and a thesaurus to see what a wide range of options the language offers. Use your judgement, though: not all apparent synonyms work well in every context.

Plan

Always begin with a plan on a single sheet. Remember that this is the plan of a sustained argument, not a list of topics. Keep the plan before you at all times.

As you develop and refine what you think in the course of writing, the plan will change. Modify the sheet immediately to make sure you're still putting a case, even if it's not the one you started with. With luck it won't be: instead, it will be much more subtle.

Revise

When you've put your argument together, read it through. Could it be sharper, clearer, more convincing? Are there gaps, contradictions, loopholes? Would *you* be persuaded? Then read it again, out loud perhaps, to hear the rhythms. Is it stylish? Always proofread to avoid annoying elementary errors.

I'm not asking you to do anything I don't do. We can't all write like Shakespeare but we can bring pleasure to a jaded examiner, and pleasure brings certain rewards. Trust me: I've been that examiner.

The confident exercise of a skill is gratifying and once you start to enjoy writing, you're getting there. Have a good time!

FURTHER READING

Some of the titles that follow are self-explanatory or mentioned in the course of the book. I have allowed these to stand alone. In other instances I have added a comment designed to indicate the particular usefulness of a specific recommendation.

General

References to *Romeo and Juliet* are to the Arden edition, ed. René Weis (London: Bloomsbury, 2012). All other Shakespeare references are to *The Arden Shakespeare Complete Works*, Richard Proudfoot, Ann Thompson and David Scott Kastan (eds) (London: Bloomsbury, 2011).

The New Casebook on *Romeo and Juliet*, ed. R. S. White (Basingstoke: Palgrave, 2001) contains a good range of essays, including those by Dympna C. Callaghan and Kiernan Ryan, as well as others I have singled out under specific headings below.

Language

Stephen Booth, 'Shakespeare's Language and the Language of Shakespeare's Time', *Shakespeare Survey 50* (1997), 1–17.

Russ McDonald, *Shakespeare and the Arts of Language* (Oxford: Oxford University Press, 2001). 'My conviction that the study of language is central to the understanding and appreciation of Shakespeare's work informs every page of this book. That belief derives from the even more basic tenet that his control of language – more than plot, characterization, theme – gives his work its distinctive qualities and underwrites his demonstrated theatrical sovereignty.' My favourite chapter is 7, 'Double Talk', 137–63.

M. M. Mahood, 'Romeo and Juliet', *Shakespeare's Wordplay* (London: Methuen, 1957), 56–72.

For a substantial history of the language, see N. F. Blake, *The Language of Shakespeare* (Basingstoke: Macmillan, 1989) but regrettably *Romeo and Juliet* does not feature prominently.

Love

On love and marriage, see Catherine Belsey, *Shakespeare and the Loss of Eden: The Construction of Family Values in Early Modern Culture* (Basingstoke: Macmillan, 1999).

While early modern moralists (and dramatists) were beginning to favour marrying for love, contemporary essayists were often sceptical: Francis Bacon, 'Of Love' [1612], *The Essays*, ed. John Pitcher (Harmondsworth: Penguin, 1985), 88–9; William Cornwallis, 'Of Love' [1600], *Essayes*, ed. Don Cameron Allen (Baltimore, MD: Johns Hopkins University Press, 1946), 20–1.

For some of the complexities of love, see Denis de Rougement, 'The Tristan Myth', *Love in the Western World*, trans. Montgomery Belgion (Princeton, NJ: Princeton University Press, 1983), 15–55; Roland Barthes, *A Lover's Discourse: Fragments* (London: Jonathan Cape, 1979), where I have quoted from 'I-love-you', 147–54; Pascal Bruckner, *The Paradox of Love*, trans. Steven Rendall (Princeton, NJ: Princeton University Press, 2012), 1–75.

Death

Julia Kristeva, 'Romeo and Juliet: Love-Hatred in the Couple', *Tales of Love* (New York: Columbia University Press, 1987), 209–25 (reprinted in R. S. White's New Casebook, 68–84).

W. H. Auden, 'Romeo and Juliet', *Lectures on Shakespeare*, ed. Arthur Kirsch (Princeton, NJ: Princeton University Press, 2000), 44–52.

Elisabeth Bronfen, 'Shakespeare's Nocturnal World', *Gothic*

Shakespeares, John Drakakis and Dale Townshend (eds) (Abingdon: Routledge, 2008), 20–41.

Carla Freccero, 'Romeo and Juliet Love Death', *Shakesqueer: A Queer Companion to the Complete Works of Shakespeare*, ed. Madhavi Menon (Durham, NC: Duke University Press, 2011), 302–8.

If you're ready for an adventure, try Jacques Derrida on the deadly potential of proper names in the play: 'Aphorism Countertime', *Acts of Literature*, ed. Derek Attridge (New York: Routledge, 1992), 414–33.

For the erotic implications of the Dance of Death (with illustrations) see Catherine Belsey, *Shakespeare and the Loss of Eden*, 140–56.

Gender

Faramerz Dabhoiwala, *The Origins of Sex: A History of the First Sexual Revolution* (London: Allen Lane, 2012), 141–79. A social historian charts the decline into opposite sexes.

For active female sexuality in the early modern period, see Helen Cooper, *The English Romance in Time: Transforming Motifs from Geoffrey of Monmouth to the Death of Shakespeare* (Oxford: Oxford University Press, 2004), 218–68.

On love's power to effeminate at the time, see Alan Sinfield, *The Wilde Century: Effeminacy, Oscar Wilde and the Queer Moment* (New York: Columbia University Press, 1994), 25–33. Stephen Orgel gives a detailed account of attitudes to boy actors and homoeroticism in 'The Eye of the Beholder', *Impersonations: The Performance of Gender in Shakespeare's England* (Cambridge: Cambridge University Press, 1996), 31–52.

On same-sex relations in the play see Joseph A. Porter, 'Friendship and Love', *Shakespeare's Mercutio: His History and Drama* (Chapel Hill: University of North Carolina Press, 1988), 145–63; Jonathan Goldberg, 'Romeo and Juliet's Open Rs', *Queering the Renaissance*, ed. Jonathan Goldberg (Durham, NC: Duke University Press, 1994), 218–35 (reprinted in R. S. White's New Casebook, 194–212); Carla Freccero, 'Romeo and Juliet Love Death', *Shakesqueer*, 302–8.

Michel Foucault, *The History of Sexuality, Volume I: An Introduction*, trans. Robert Hurley (London: Allen Lane, 1979). I have quoted p. 43.

Alan Bray's *Homosexuality in Renaissance England* (London: Gay Men's Press, 1982) is informative and readable. His *The Friend* (Chicago, IL: University of Chicago Press, 2003) is unsurpassed but more demanding.

Sources

Arthur Brooke, *Romeus and Juliet* (1562, 1587) is available online in a reliable modernized edition at http://www.shakespeare-navigators.com/romeo/BrookeIndex.html [accessed 6 August 2013]. This is helpfully divided with individual synopses, so that it is easy to use.

A modernized version of William Painter, 'Romeo and Julietta' (1567, 1580) is included in T. J. B. Spencer, ed., *Elizabethan Love Stories* (Harmondsworth: Penguin, 1968), 51–96.

Shakespeare's schooling in Latin literature is everywhere apparent in his writing. Ovid is surprisingly readable. You can find the story of Tiresias, who had been both man and woman, in Ovid's *Metamorphoses*, 3.318–33. The tale of Pyramus and Thisbe is told in 4.55–166 (and burlesqued in *A Midsummer Night's Dream*, 5.1.126–342). For the myth of Phaeton, see 2.1–332. Various translations of Ovid are available. I'd go for unassuming modern prose in the first instance.

Virgil's tragic story of Dido and Aeneas also contributes indirectly the play and to much of Shakespeare's work. You can find it in *Aeneid*, 4. Again, I'd choose a modern prose translation.

Shakespeare's stage

John H. Astington, *Actors and Acting in Shakespeare's Time: The Art of Stage Playing* (Cambridge: Cambridge University Press, 2010).

Andrew Gurr, *The Shakespeare Company, 1594–1642* (Cambridge: Cambridge University Press, 2004).

Editing

Most modern editions are based on Q2. You can find a photographic facsimile of the first printed version of this at: http://internetshakespeare.uvic.ca/Library/facsimile/book/BL_Q2_Rom/1/?zoom=1 [accessed 6 August 2013].

A comparable facsimile of Q1 is available in Arden 3. Jill Levenson's edition of *Romeo and Juliet* (Oxford: Oxford University Press, 2000) includes a modern-spelling version. Lukas Erne's modern-spelling edition of Q1 (Cambridge: Cambridge University Press, 2007) contains an introduction explaining his theory of the difference between Q1 as an imperfect record of performance and Q2 as a reading version.

But the best way to compare Q1 and Q2 is to see them side by side. Jay Halio has edited a modern-spelling *Romeo and Juliet: Parallel Texts of Quarto 1 (1597) and Quarto 2 (1599)* (Newark: University of Delaware Press, 2008) but errors of transcription and editorial interventions diminish its usefulness. If you can cope with old spelling, an older but more reliable version is available at: http://archive.org/stream/romeojulietparal00shakuoft#page/n0/mode/2up [accessed 6 August 2013].

For a brief account of the printing process, including a picture of an early modern printing press, see Russ McDonald, *The Bedford Companion to Shakespeare* (New York: St Martin's Press; Basingstoke: Macmillan, 1996), 74–99.

Paul Werstine's challenge to the story of good and bad quartos (*Shakespeare Quarterly*, 41 (1990), 65–86) is reprinted in Russ McDonald, ed., *Shakespeare: An Anthology of Criticism and Theory 1945–2000* (Oxford: Blackwell, 2004), 296–317.

There is a wealth of material in Andrew Murphy, ed., *A Concise Companion to Shakespeare and the Text* (Oxford: Blackwell, 2007), including valuable essays by Thomas L. Berger, Paul Werstine, and Leah S. Marcus.

Afterlives

Jill Levenson gives a chronological account of the most influential or outstanding productions of the play in *Romeo and Juliet*, Shakespeare in Performance (Manchester: Manchester University Press, 1987).

Alan C. Dessen has written widely about the differences between current performance and early modern stage practices. Here I have cited *Rescripting Shakespeare: The Text, the Director, and Modern Productions* (Cambridge: Cambridge University Press, 2002), 6, 17.

Thomas Otway's *The History and Fall of Caius Marius*, published in 1680, as well as the adaptations of *Romeo and Juliet* by Theophilus Cibber and David Garrick are available in facsimile editions of the original texts of 1748 and 1750 (all London: Cornmarket Press, 1969).

Adrian Poole, *Shakespeare and the Victorians*, The Arden Critical Companions (London: Thomson Learning, 2004) is a valuable resource. Use the index if you want to confine your attention to *Romeo and Juliet*.

Lisa Merrill, *When Romeo Was a Woman: Charlotte Cushman and her Circle of Female Spectators* (Ann Arbor: University of Michigan Press, 1999), 110–37.

There are nuggets to be found in Ann Thompson, ed., *Women Reading Shakespeare, 1600–1900: An Anthology* (Manchester: Manchester University Press, 1997), including an extract from Elizabeth Griffith's book (p. 33).

Barbara Hodgdon offers an astute reading of Baz Luhrmann's film in '*William Shakespeare's Romeo + Juliet*: Everything's Nice in America?' *Shakespeare Survey*, 52 (1999), 88–98. Reprinted in R. S. White's New Casebook, 129–46.